THE WOUND OF GREECE

THE WOUND
OF
GREECE

STUDIES IN NEO-HELLENISM

Philip Sherrard

Ὅπου καὶ νὰ ταξιδέψω, ἡ Ἑλλάδα μὲ πληγώνει.

George Seferis

ST MARTINS PRESS, NEW YORK 1979

Library of Congress Cataloging in Publication Data
Sherrard, Philip
   The Wound of Greece.

   Bibliography: p.
   Includes index.
   1. Civilization, Greek. 2. Greek literature, Modern
—History and criticism. I. Title.
DF78.S54   1979   938   78-27758
ISBN 0-312-8900-0

For
George Katsimbalis
A token of long friendship

ACKNOWLEDGEMENTS

Acknowledgements are due to the editors of *Byzantine and Modern Greek Studies*, *Review of National Literatures*, *London Magazine* and to John Murray, publishers of *The Pursuit of Greece*, for permission to re-use material which first appeared in the publications specified.

Contents

Contents

INTRODUCTION
Who are the Greeks?

'AS THE SAPPHIRE and the aquamarine from the turquoise, so differ the waters of the Aegean from the flat blue of the Mediterranean whole.' Thus, some years before World War II, wrote Robert Byron.[1] And he continues: 'Sail from Italy or Egypt. And as the rose-tinted shores of islands and promontories rise incarnate from the sea, a door shuts the world behind. Earth's emotion diffuses a new essence. . . . What magnet to our stifled love hold this blue, these tawny cliffs and always the mountains framing the distance? Why does the breeze blow with a scent of baking herbs which the misty shores echo in their colours? What is this element, hybrid of air and water, physical as a kiss, with which the night enfolds us?'

Some fifty or sixty years ago, such questions as these would have been entirely rhetorical. It would have been quite clear what magnet held our stifled love, why the wind blew thus and not otherwise, and what element unfolded us at night. For Greece was that most sacred of all countries, the land of gods and heroes, the land which had given birth to our civilization, to liberty, enlightenment, democracy, the arts, the sciences, rationalism, and to everything else of value:

> Where'er we tread, 'tis haunted, holy ground;
> No earth of thine is lost in vulgar mould,
> But one vast realm of Wonder spreads around,
> And all the Muse's tales seem truly told,
> Till the sense aches with gazing to behold
> The scenes our earliest dreams have dwelt upon.[2]

1

Such dreams are very powerful. And this one of the glory that was Greece, the dream of the classical Greece, has been one of the most powerful in the minds of cultured Europeans during the late humanist, Renaissance and post-Renaissance phases of our history. At about the beginning of this century, another English traveller, H. W. Nevinson, fair specimen of the cultured European, came to Greece. He arrived one afternoon and straight away made for the Acropolis of Athens, the centre of this antique glory. Unfortunately he was a bit late, the gates were closed, and though he rattled and called, no one came to let him in. So, with the sun going down behind 'Parnes and Citheron', he seated himself on one of the marble steps before the entrance, and 'I tried to realize', he wrote, 'that I was present at the very centre and supreme height of human greatness. Around this very rock the mind of man once rose to a degree of wisdom, conduct, and beauty unsurpassed in any other part of the world. . . .'[3]

For such people as these the dream of the Greece of the golden age was absolute. It filled the whole field of vision. It excluded everything but itself. That is why those questions would have been rhetorical. Greece was 'the very centre and supreme height of human greatness', and it would have been impossible for its atmosphere not to be charged with miracle and magic.

But during the last few decades those questions have ceased to be entirely rhetorical. The classical dream has ceased to be absolute. The mirage has broken. Indeed, some have begun to wonder what precise connection the Greece of the classical studies has with any historical reality. 'It is vain and foolish to talk of knowing Greek,' wrote Virginia Woolf,

> since in our ignorance we should be at the bottom of any class of schoolboys, since we do not know how the words sounded, or where precisely we ought to laugh, or how the actors acted. . . . When we read a stanza in a chorus, the end or opening of a dialogue of Plato's, a fragment of Sappho, when we bruise our minds upon some tremendous metaphor in the *Agamemnon* instead of stripping the branch of its flowers

2

instantly as we do in reading *Lear*, are we not reading wrongly, losing our sharp sight in the haze of associations? Reading into Greek poetry not what they have but what we lack? Does not the whole of Greece heap itself behind every line of its literature? They admit us to a vision of the earth unravaged, the sea unpolluted, the maturity, tried but unbroken, of mankind. . . . Back and back we are drawn to steep ourselves in what, perhaps, is only an image of the reality, not the reality itself, a summer's day imagined in the heart of a northern winter.[4]

And Robert Byron is even more critical of this unreal image and its author, the classical scholar, this

student, ultimately interpreter, of Greek texts; endowed with a kindred love of exact reasoning and exact representation, together with a kindred absence of historical perspective and emotional outlet; he has fabricated from literature and stones an ideal of humanity, which he and his followers have pronounced applicable to eternity. It is the singular odium of this eternal comparison, for centuries the bane of European culture, which necessitates, once and for all, the relegation of classicism to its just place in the tale of human development.[5]

What is evident from this is that somewhere during the last fifty-odd years the dream of the classical Greece has lost its hold; that a shift has taken place in the attitude with which Greece is regarded, with which the traveller approaches her shores. What is this shift and how has it come about? This is quite a long story, and means going back to the beginning, to show how the classical dream was built up in the first place, so that it acquired the hold it did.

One of the things which become clear when one reads the poets or dramatists of ancient Greece—and I have in mind particularly Homer, Aeschylus, and Sophocles—is that the world they deal with is for them immensely real and living. The gods, the supernatural beings that so frequently appear and direct man's life and thought, were not for them, as they may be for us, mere figments of the imagination, poetic invention, and so on. They are living dynamic forces, terrible, often terrifying realities. When Homer's heroes appeal to the gods, and Orestes, seeing the Furies unleashed and on his trail, cries 'You do not see these beings, but I see them. They are hunting me down', they are not speaking of mere allegorical figures. They are revealing and expressing the inner movement and operation of cosmic powers in certain concrete situations. And this sense of the activity of such powers seems to pervade the whole of life. The gods are active in nature itself, in natural and human relationships: they are a way of life, an attestation of life—not effigies, illusions, or inventions. And the great effort of the great poets of ancient Greece was to reveal and express, from the interior to the exterior, the reality, movement, and compulsion of this god-haunted, god-tormented universe in which they lived. There was an immediate, urgent and vital connection between literature and life. The poet's function was not simply to amuse or decorate: it was to speak of what was of the utmost importance for a man to know; and to speak of it in a way, in a language that man could understand—in a language which was itself living and real, the actual language of the people among whom the poet lived.

This intimate connection between literature and life was gradually lost. Literature ceased to be an expression of life, of an experienced reality, and became something else. When, following the conquests of Alexander the Great, that world known as the Hellenistic world emerged, its chief centres were those commercial agglomerations like Alexandria, Antioch and Ephesus which studded the whole Middle-Eastern area. These cities were rather like new towns of today. They were laid out on the lines of the cities of ancient Greece, but laid out as it were *in vacuo*. They were culturally rootless, with no local traditions of their own. But they were the outcome of the Greek *diaspora*, and their main language was Greek. So that when it became a question of trying to fill the vacuum, or trying to find something to make up for their lack of native cultural roots, it was only natural that they should look back to ancient Greece. In the literature of ancient Greece the citizens of these Hellenistic cities sought the cultural basis for their own civilization. They sought to

4

imitate the models provided by ancient Greece, and to mould their world according to the patterns of fifth-century Athens. They adopted the language of the past, they tried to think in categories of the past, to fit their lives into the framework of a bygone, outmoded age. They wanted their epics and hymns to be like those of Homer, their prose like that of their Attic models. They produced glossaries of difficult poetic words, glossaries of Homer, systematic grammars, vast tomes on Attic metaphors and on comic and tragic diction. What in fact they were trying to do was to fashion a perfect instrument for the imitation of those classical models which they regarded as the ideal forms of culture, of civilization itself. The more perfect they could make this instrument, the more completely they would be able to conform life and thought to those Attic prototypes which they so venerated.

This imitative habit, this cult of the classical past, continued with the Romans. Rome took over the classical heritage in its Hellenistic form. More and more did literature cease to be a direct expression of life, and more and more did it aspire to be but a copy of past literary models. Its language became ever more remote from ordinary speech, and ever more a matter of artistic convention and scholarship, derivative and pedantic. In this way the last centuries of the Roman Empire saw those imitative tendencies which had characterized all literature since the death of Alexander the Great developed to an unprecedented degree. Life and literature had fallen apart. Literature had degenerated into being little more than the instrument of classical education, the means whereby that Procrustean operation of forcing life into the classical mould could be most effectively performed. At the same time, as a counterpart to this process, the image of the ancient Greek world itself became more and more abstract, atrophied and artificial. Cut off from its living roots; divorced from all historical reality; set apart from the present; its gods turned into vacuous man-made effigies, effete literary fictions or devices of a dream-like etiolated prettiness, ancient Greece became a kind of lost paradise, a great golden past in which souls too timid or trivial for

5

anything else could find relief from the horrors and afflictions of contemporary megalopolitan life.

The next landmark in this story is the Renaissance. At the time of the Renaissance, this 'classicism' was 'reborn'. Why was this? Renaissance man, it is commonly said, is an individualist. The individualism of the Renaissance—not incidentally, a sudden growth, but one going back through the Middle Ages to the Hellenistic world—this individualism represented a revolt against Christian thought and the type of society that goes with it: a more corporate, impersonal, and hierarchic type of society than that demanded by the Renaissance man. But this revolt had to find a cultural and ideological basis somewhere, just as the Hellenistic world had to find such a basis somewhere. And as the Hellenistic world looked back to ancient Greece for this basis, so the Renaissance humanists in their turn looked back, not to ancient Greece (as they might have thought they were looking back), but to the form which the literature and thought of ancient Greece had been given in Hellenistic and Roman times. Hence their cry of 'back to the classics'. In the classics were thought to be embodied the values according to which Renaissance man desired to live. They were to be the models for the new civilization which was just emerging, the new humanist world. Imitate the classics and all would be well. So far did this attitude develop that Petrarch, for instance, typical of the new mentality, laid it down that only Greek and Latin were suitable languages for literature. Only Greek and Latin authors should be read for guidance on how to live, how to enjoy nature, how to cultivate friendship, and so on. Thus, imitation and ideological interests went together, and the great work of providing modern European civilization with its cultural basis had begun.

There was another aspect to this undertaking. The classics were to serve as models for the new humanist way of life. Well and good. But to gather the classics together, to prepare and edit them for printing, to produce them in such a way that their language and structure could be adopted for current literary use—this was an enormous task. It needed a

6

considerable degree of learning, an elaborate technical knowledge. These were things that not everyone possessed or could acquire. Only a few could master them—a small select company of scholars, of finely trained classical experts. Hence the enormous prestige attaching to classical scholarship from the very foundation of our modern western civilization, for it was the classical scholars who had to perform the task of providing this civilization with its intellectual and cultural models in a form that could be assimilated.[6]

By the end of the sixteenth century the classical scholars had in fact fulfilled their creative role—that of giving a cultural basis to the middle-class revolution of the Renaissance. Classicism had by then become the possession of popular writers and was no longer the privileged reserve of scholars. It had become embedded, even fossilized, in those most stubborn and recalcitrant of all institutions, the schools and universities of Europe. From now on classical scholars could bask in reflected glory, enjoy a status and an esteem not for the work they were now doing but for the work which their pioneering predecessors had done a century or two before. The work they were now doing and were to do for the next few centuries had none of this pioneering or creative quality. More and more it was devoted to the mere gathering of information about the ancient world and its goings-on, and to filing this information in fat handbooks (or more recently in diminutive articles) where those who wished could get at it with the least possible bother. It was a task of preservation and diffusion: of trying to maintain the classical discipline and of propagating its ideals among the new mercantile classes, of remoulding the taste of the educated European so that it conformed to these ideals—was, that is, non-religious, rational, materialist, and looked back to the ancient world and in particular to fifth-century Athens as both the cradle and the great period of the arts, the sciences, of civilization itself.

How well they performed their task may be gathered from the emergence, under their direct influence, of a new type of humanism. This was the humanism of those who had made

7

good in the new bourgeois world of modern Europe, had grown rich and possibly picked up a title in the process, had imbibed through education the classical taste, and who were now consequently in a financial and cultural condition to indulge this taste in a way which flattered their own vanity and was in harmony with the finest ideals of civilization. This new humanism was not that of scholars and schoolmasters, of universities and schools. It was that of learned societies and dilettante gentlemen. Its adepts preferred the gathering of objects to the gathering of information, preferred coins, statues, vases and inscriptions to the annotation of texts and the compiling of dictionaries. Addison the essayist discussed the relevance of coins to literary criticism; and Gibbon, escaping from Oxford, spent £20 on 20 volumes of the *Memoirs of the Academy of Inscriptions.*

Above all these new humanist gentlemen liked travel. Italy was still of course the main centre of the European tour, since it was relatively accessible and was in addition the scene of the extraordinary discoveries at Herculaneum and Pompeii. But the fortunate few ventured further afield. The fortunate few got as far as Greece. And here the wheel came full circle. Here, in a way, Greek met Greek—the humanist, nourished on the classics, considering himself the latest, and finest, flower of the classical tradition, came back to the place where, as he thought, it had all started, to the native land of the Greeks. And here precisely was the rub.

It was towards the end of the eighteenth and beginning of the nineteenth centuries that these gentlemen travellers began to reach Greece in any number, at a time when the Greek people were preparing for their War of Independence from the Turks. It was the age of Romanticism, of new ideas about liberty and nationality. The Greek cause caught the imagination. It seemed to combine everything: all the classical associations, the struggle for freedom, the rights of nations. The country which had given birth to European civilization—which was taken to be the only civilization there was—was at last itself going to be reborn. The wheel, as was said, had come full circle; and many were the romantic philhellenes who took up the Greek cause. Shelley was one of them. In his preface to his drama, *Hellas*, published in 1822, he expresses perfectly the romantic philhellenes' state of mind:

> The apathy of the rulers of the civilized world to the astonishing circumstances of the descendants of that nation to which they owe their civilization—rising as it were from the ashes of their ruin, is something perfectly inexplicable to a mere spectator of the shews of this mortal scene. We are all Greeks. Our laws, our literature, our religion, our arts, have their root in Greece. . . . The human form and the human mind attained to a perfection in Greece. . . . The modern Greek is the descendant of those glorious beings whom the imagination almost refuses to figure to itself as belonging to our kind . . .

And in the final chorus of the drama he sings of this reborn Greece:

> The world's great age begins anew,
> The golden years return,
> The earth doth like a snake renew
> Her winter weeds outworn. . . .
>
> A brighter Hellas rears its mountains
> From waves serener far;
> A new Peneus rolls his fountains
> Against the morning-star. . . .
>
> Another Athens shall arise . . .

This might go unchallenged as long as one didn't visit Greece or know too much about the modern Greeks. But if one did go, as our humanist gentlemen, Byron among them, went, then things were more difficult. For the image of Greece these gentlemen carried with them was that artificial image enshrined in the classical tradition which they had received from their preceptors at various establishments of higher learning. Greece was the land of sylvan nymphs and piping shepherds, of the great god Pan down by the river, of old Triton blowing his horn, of islands where burning Sapphos sang, of Arcadia and straight noses. This image, in

9

spite (or perhaps because) of its lack of connection with any historical reality, was for those travellers at the end of the eighteenth and beginning of the nineteenth centuries extremely real. And the rub came because the historical reality of Greece at this same period was anything but classical. Thus, on the one hand there was the legend-wrapped Greek, descendant of his half-divine ancestors, now once again in the forefront of the battle for freedom and justice—'hereditary bondsman' still, but son of the heroes of Thermopylae and Salamis; and on the other hand there was the Greek of flesh and blood, probably entirely ignorant of the heroes of Thermopylae and Salamis, member perhaps of some wild Peloponnesian tribe, and to all intents and purposes conspicuously lacking in those virtues and features with which centuries of classical legend had encrusted the ancient Greek. He wasn't rational. He wasn't enlightened. He knew little of his ancestors and cared less for their monuments. And worst of all, his life and its activities were vilified by his subscription to a religion which he had inherited directly from that Christian Byzantium which to the humanists (suckled on the inane maledictions of their Gibbon) stood for practically everything that was non-classical, obscurantist, barbarous, of the Dark Ages. The world of the Greek revival received the news of this discrepancy between the ancient and modern Greeks with an ill-concealed sense of pain and bewilderment. If the members of this world were themselves Greeks—as, with Shelley, they were quite sure they were—how could the modern Greeks be Greek, or even have anything to do with glorious Hellas?

It was not long before an answer was found. It was a remarkably simple answer: the modern Greeks were not Greeks. Or at most very few of them were Greeks. The majority was Slav or, more precisely, Albanian. 'The Albanian race occupies no inconsiderable portion of ancient Greece', wrote the historian Finlay;[7] and he goes on to specify where these Albanian colonists have settled: all Attica and Megara, the greater part of Boeotia, parts of Locris, Andros, and Euboea; Marathon, Plataea, Salamis,

Mantinea, Olympia; Poros, Hydra, Spetsai, and so on: practically the whole of Greece. Many of the famous so-called 'Greek' heroes of the War of Independence were, we are told, really Albanians. Even the 'national' Greek dress—the fustanella—is in fact the dress of one of the great Albanian tribes, the Tosks, and was adopted only after the War of Independence in recognition of the warlike virtues of the Albanians, though, Finlay adds, 'the calico fustanella hangs round the legs of the Greeks like a paper petticoat, while the white kilt of the Tosk, formed from a strong product of native looms, fell in the graceful folds of *antique* drapery'[8]—the implication being that at least the Albanians had some connection with ancient Greece, even if the modern Greeks had none. All this, ably supported by the researches of the German scholar Fallmerayer, was a great relief. The descendants of Pericles and Phidias were dead, and those living beneath the broken stumps of the Parthenon were 'the unmoral refuse of mediaeval Slav migrations, sullying the land of their birth with the fury of their politics, and the malformation of their small brown bodies.'[9]

Thus the good classicist could breathe again; could, oblivious of Adam's fall, go on measuring his walls and gathering his sherds without having to worry himself about whether the mirage in whose name ultimately he performed these jejune activities was really more than the product of a stunted imagination. But in fact the release was only temporary. By the end of the nineteenth century other winds were abroad, threatening and disruptive, signs of the beginning of the shift spoken of at the start of this intro-duction. First, the classical idea of ancient Greece itself began to be doubted. It was felt that the ancients may have been far less rational and enlightened than imagined. Behind the classical poise, dark and uncontrollable forces were dis-cerned—Dionysiac forces, mysteries and orgies, strange rites, sexual and savage, a vast irrational chthonic world. Irrational but vital. Religious but creative. Nietzsche went as far as to say that Greek decadence set in with the classical period, when the reason began to cripple and deny the

11

expression of the dark forces. And as if to confirm this, archaic sculpture began to be unearthed—sculpture beside which the classical mode seemed flaccid and vacuous. In addition, there were the excavations of Schliemann at Mycenae and Troy, and a little later, after the turn of the century, those of Evans at Knossos. The image of ancient Greece suddenly became more complex, harder to fit into the classical framework.

Then, the appalling ugliness of the huge industrial world being built up in the West, and particularly in England, in the nineteenth century—a world from which art seemed to be more and more excluded, in which it seemed increasingly separated from life and society—made several people wonder when this sundering of art and life first began to take place; and as they saw it, it first began to take place with the revival of the classical tradition at the time of the Renaissance. Already Blake had written: 'The Classics! it is the Classics, and not Goths nor monks, that desolate Europe with Wars.' And the counterpart to the enquiry into when art and life in modern England had fallen apart was a returning for inspiration to an epoch in which they still seemed to inter-penetrate and coalesce. This epoch was identified with the pre-Raphaelite period, the mediaeval period. Those leading this enquiry began to find their models in this period, in the Christian art and life of the Middle Ages so abused by Gibbon and his like. But searching in and behind these models they began to discern the outlines and influences of Byzantium and Byzantine art. Mostly it was what outlines and influences they could discern in Italy—at Venice, Ravenna, or in Sicily. Burne-Jones visited Ravenna in 1873 to see its 'heavenly churches'—churches which, it may be remembered, had made no impression on Shelley or Byron some six decades earlier. Burne-Jones himself designed mosaics; the revival of mosaics was part of that general 'revival' of the arts centring round William Morris and his followers. Both Oscar Wilde and Arthur Symons visited Ravenna and wrote about Byzantine art. In 1894, Lethaby and Swainson published the first serious study of St Sophia, 'the most interesting building on the world's surface', as they called it;[10] and in 1912 Dalton published his work on Byzantine art.[11] A breach had at last been made in that asphyxiating world of classical preconceptions to which since the time of the Renaissance the theory and practice of the arts had for the most part been confined.

Thirdly, the persistent presence of a contemporary people, Slav migrants or not, living in the land of Greece, speaking the Greek language and possessing a wealth of custom and belief in which classical scholars themselves perceived overtones and undertones of ancient myth and religious practice, was something that couldn't be written off for ever as essentially unrelated to the Greek scene. To start with, if an unmixed genealogy was to be the criterion of what constitutes a people, then no one would come off very well, least of all the English. In fact, the identity of a people depends on more subtle factors than this: depends on common ways of thought and feeling, on common assumptions and attitudes, on common religious beliefs and practices. And here, for what it was worth, the modern Greeks could claim a far greater continuity of inheritance from the ancient Greek world than could their western detractors. In a sense, this has been partially at least their misfortune, for many of them, putting themselves too readily and uncritically to learn at western schools, have themselves become victims of the classical image of antiquity (which they now regard as *their* antiquity), a lapse which has led, and still leads, to many abuses and confusions, often at the expense of what is of value and beauty in their own proper tradition. But this apart, the fact that on closer acquaintance the modern Greeks were discovered to possess certain qualities and characteristics to which parallels could be found in the writings of ancient authors meant that it was impossible to dismiss them altogether as having nothing to do with their so-called ancestors; but on the other hand, the fact that they so desperately failed to conform in so many other ways to the classical ideal of humanity meant that, if they couldn't be dismissed, some adjustment might have to be made to this

13

ideal itself. In other words, it began to become evident that instead of the classical yardstick being used to measure the degree of the 'Greekness' of anything, including the modern Greeks, some other standard of what constitutes the essence of Hellenism would have to be found, one to which the classical artifice whose history we have been tracing would itself have to give way.

All this soon began to have its effects. We have already noted Virginia Woolf doubting whether the classical image of Greece was anything but a dream; and the new perspectives of ancient Greek history and art being opened up, those of the archaic period and, further back, of Knossos, were influencing the minds of creative writers like D. H. Lawrence:

> Little islands out at sea, on the horizon
> keep suddenly showing a whiteness, a flash and a furl, a hail
> of something coming, ships a-sail from over the rim of the sea.
>
> And every time it is ships, it is ships—
> it is ships of Cnossos coming, out of the morning and the sea,
> it is Aegean ships, and men with archaic pointed beards
> coming out of the Eastern end . . .[12]

At the same time, the measure of the impact of Byzantine Greece can be gauged by the fact that while Byzantium has no place—as far as I am aware—in the imaginative world of English romantic poets like Keats and Shelley, it is at the very centre of the imaginative world of such a poet as W. B. Yeats, who in two of his greatest poems chose Byzantium as the only fit symbol for the profound and compound meaning he wished to convey, and who regarded early Byzantium as the most complete example known to recorded history of that supreme type of society in which religious, aesthetic and practical life were one. And more recently writers such as Lawrence Durrell have sought to penetrate into the living landscape of Greece itself and to grasp its mystery and power:

> Greece: the vertical, masculine adventurous consciousness of

14

the archipelago, with its mental anarchy and indiscipline touched everywhere with the taste of agnosticism and spare living: Greece born into the sexual intoxication of the light, which seems to shine upwards from inside the very earth, to illuminate those bare acres of squill and asphodel.[13]

The result is that the image of Greece has now assumed new dimensions, a new complexity. The Greece of the classical heritage and of the romantic philhellene has gone, and anyhow has always been irrelevant to the Greek situation. Greece is not and never has been a lost paradise or a haven for tourists or an object of study, and those who approach her as if she were any of these will always fail to make any real contact with her. For to achieve this it is not enough to act in the manner of those who singly or in droves are to be seen pouring exhaustively and exhaustingly over the Greek landscape, guide-book or notebook in one hand, camera or tape-measure in the other, hurrying from site to site, from island to island, pausing here to observe the niceness of the view, there the shortcomings of the food or drainage, elsewhere how graced with or delightfully free from western virtues the natives are; for this is merely an avoidance of experience or understanding. He who would wish for these must have a more receptive and unhurried kind of temperament, one that is able to let things be what they are and to express their own natures rather than serve as the raw material for some purpose or other, be it only one's own pleasure. He must have sought out not the past but the living fate of Greece, which is not a doom but a destiny, a process rather in which past and present blend and fuse, in which nature and man and something more than man participate: a process difficult, baffling, enigmatic, with its element of magic, its element of tragedy, working itself out in a landscape of bare hills and insatiable sea, in the miraculous cruelty of the summer sun, in the long generations of the lives of the Greek people. The following essays are an attempt, not indeed to define this destiny or this process (for that is impossible), but to indicate, through the lives and writings of Greeks themselves, something of its quality, as well as of the complexity of the forces—historical, cultural, social—which have helped to shape it.

Andreas Kalvos and
The Eighteenth-Century Ethos

IN THE SPACE of a few years the small isle of Zante, one of the Ionian group, produced three important poets: Hugo Foscolo, Dionysios Solomos and the subject of this study, Andreas Kalvos. Kalvos was born in 1792, fourteen years after Foscolo and six years before Solomos.[1] His father's family may originally have come from Crete. His mother's family was one of the aristocratic families of Zante—the family name had been inscribed, ever since the Venetian occupation of the island, in the Gold Book of the island nobility. The marriage of the poet's parents does not seem to have been a success, for not many years after the birth of his younger brother in 1794, the father, taking the two children with him, left Zante for Leghorn, where his brother was consul for the Ionian Islands and where there was a considerable Greek colony. In 1805, Andreas' mother obtained a divorce from her husband on the grounds of desertion, and shortly afterwards she married for the second time. She died in 1815, never having seen her children again after their departure from Zante.

Little is known of Kalvos' early life in Italy. But a youthful apprenticeship to the difficult craft of poetry is made evident by the fact that in 1811 he wrote, in Italian, an ode 'To Napoleon' (his hero was still regarded as the great deliverer of the people of Europe from the chains of slavery and oppression). We really only pick up the threads of his life again in 1813, when he became tutor at Florence to a ward of Hugo Foscolo. It was now that the important association of the two poets began, an association which was to be, from Kalvos' point of view, both stimulating and frustrating.

17

From the beginning Foscolo seems to have assumed a somewhat patronizing attitude in his relationship with his young protégé. He set himself up as his mentor and put him through a long course of classical studies. Under Foscolo's influence and under the influence of his newly acquired classical learning, Kalvos wrote, again in Italian, two tragedies, *Thiramenis* and *The Danaides*. Neither of these two works does more than imitate the example of Kalvos' master and in general that of other Italian writers like Alfieri, and neither has any intrinsic literary value.

In 1815 Foscolo was forced to leave Florence because of his 'advanced' ideas, and he took refuge in Switzerland. For a year Kàlvos remained by himself in Florence, where he again became a teacher, and where he wrote his second Italian ode, 'To the Ionians', which is interesting only because it reveals that the poet, even at this stage and in spite of his adopted Italian, was nevertheless deeply conscious of his own country and of her plight. It was also during this period that Rousseau began to occupy a special place in Kalvos' philosophical and aesthetic reading. Then in 1816 he left Florence to join Foscolo in Switzerland, breaking up, it seems, a love-affair with a Jewish woman for the purpose. In the same year the two poets journeyed to London. There, a few months later, they quarrelled and separated. The precise reasons for the quarrel are not known and in any case need not detain us. It is enough to say that Foscolo later accused Kalvos of having exploited him, accepting his keep and counsel without return. Kalvos is silent about the whole affair. It seems likely, however, that the younger poet began to tire of his relationship with the elder; that he began to find the atmosphere too constricting, and that he felt the need to break away and establish his independence from the patronizing and probably somewhat possessive companionship of Foscolo. After the separation, Kalvos continued to live in London, earning his living by giving Italian and Greek lessons and by translating religious propaganda such as the *Liturgia Anglicana Polyglotta*. He seems in fact to have become quite an authority on religious questions, on which he also wrote articles and gave lectures. After what seems to have been a succession of love-affairs, he married and had a daughter. Both wife and daughter died a few years later.

In 1821 Kalvos returned to Florence. His association with Foscolo, however, had made him politically suspect in the eyes of the authorities, and he was forced to go once more to Switzerland. There he came into contact with enthusiastic philhellenic circles. The date coincides with the outbreak of the Greek War of Independence. All the hopes and fears, ideals and enthusiasms which for years had been maturing in the heart of the Greek people came to a head and exploded. In 1824 Kalvos published his first ten Greek odes which, together with his second volume of a further ten odes, published in 1826, form one long hymn to Greece and to Greek freedom. These twenty odes were all he wrote in Greek: his first song was his swansong. In 1826 Kalvos left Switzerland for Greece, in order, as he writes in the dedication of his second volume of odes to General Lafayette, to *'exposer un coeur de plus au feu de Musulmans'*.

The phrase was rhetorical, but it expressed a genuine expectation and a genuine intention. Kalvos, when he left Switzerland, had no doubt hoped to find in Greece and to give his services to men who were the reincarnation of the ancient heroes of Marathon and of Salamis as seen through the distorting mirror of an idealizing classical tradition. No doubt he had hoped to receive welcome as a new Byron, ready to sacrifice his life on the altar of Greek freedom. He landed in Navplia. His imaginary heroes he found to be but flesh-and-blood creatures, rough, unlearned and obstinate, who, if they performed acts of astonishing courage and daring, yet resented the presence of 'foreigners'—and Kalvos, although a Greek, was from their point of view a foreigner; who if they could at times sacrifice themselves without hesitation to their country, at other times were full of rival jealousies and hatreds. To Kalvos, who had expected something very different, their appearance must have been as disillusioning as the appearance of the strange and terrible Greek sailors to the philhellene Shelley.[2] Far from being crowned as his country's new Tyrtaeus, Kalvos was ignored. It may have been the shock of finding himself so out of contact with the Revolution and with the Revolutionaries whose ideals he had sung with such fervour that induced him to retreat. In any case, he soon left for Corfu, to the welcome of, among others, Lord Guilford of the Ionian Academy. There he found an atmosphere more congenial to his temperament. But the poet in him appears to have suffered some injury beyond cure. Kàlvos died, in England, in 1869. During the forty-three years between 1826—when he published his second volume of odes—and the day of his death, he did not write, as far as is known, a single further line of poetry.

This brief account of Kalvos' life serves as an approach to his poetry. This approach is not altogether easy. Kalvos' poetry has many characteristics which, as it were, prevent one from coming into contact with it, or at least prevent one from estimating its worth. It possesses in fact a dual or even a triple personality; and only after one has learnt to distinguish what is false in it, and why it is false, can one give it the real sympathy and attention that poetry demands. Take for instance the following poem, the first of his twenty odes, a hymn to his native island Zante which he left when still a young child:

The Patriot

Beloved homeland,
isle of wonder,
Zante, you gave me
breath and Apollo's gift.

Accept the praise:
the gods hate the soul
of the ungrateful
and thunder above their heads.

Never shall I forget you,
never—though fate
far from you has flung me:
for twenty-five years have I been
    in strange countries.

But glad or miserable
when light enriches
mountain and wave
I set you always before my eyes.

When night with her pitch-black veil
covers
the sky's roses,
you are the one happiness of my dreams.

Once the sun lit my steps
on the blessed
Ausonian earth; there
clear air laughs always.

There the people rejoice;
there Parnassian girls
dance and the sacred
leaf crowns the lyre.

Wild and huge run
the seas; with violence
they pound and rend themselves upon
Albion's rocks.

Power and glory,
abundant wealth,
are unloaded
on the shores of the clear Thames.

There the Aeolian breath
brought me; rays
of sweetest freedom
nourished and cured me.

And I admired your temples,
holy Celtic city;
what beauty, of thought, of spirit,
can you lack?

Farewell, Ausonia, farewell
Albion and glorious Paris;
lovely and alone, Zante
rules me.

Zakynthian woods,
her shaded hills
echoed once
with the silver bows of Artemis.

And now shepherds
still worship the trees
and the cool springs;
Nereids still haunt them.

The Ionian wave
first kissed the body,
first the Ionian breeze caressed the breasts
of Cytherea.

And when the evening star
glows in the sky
and ships sail
full of love and singing,

then the same wave kisses,
the same breeze caresses
the body and breasts
of white Zakynthian girls.

Delicious your air,
beloved homeland,
enriching the sea
with the scent of gold lemons.

The king of the gods gave you
grape-bearing roots,
gave you bright, clear,
diaphanous clouds.

Eternal light
rains on your fruit by day,
and for you
night's tears become lilies.

If it falls, the snow
melts from your face,
hot summer
never dulls your emeralds.

Happy you are; and more
happy I call you
because you have never known
the harsh whip of tyrants.

Let my fate not give me
a tomb on a strange shore;
death is sweet only
when we sleep in our own land.

Contemporary sensibility, once it has accepted the convention in which this poem is written, will not have much difficulty in responding to it, in responding to the pure lyric expression of a wanderer's love for his birth-place and his native land. The formal opening of the first two stanzas gives place quite naturally to the straightforward statement of a personal relationship in stanzas 3 to 5. In stanzas 6 to 12, where the motif of absence is expanded, one enters a dead patch; the passage is stylized, pedantic and clumsy in its use of classical names; the poem is marking time, if not wasting time, and nothing would be lost if the verses were cut out—they add nothing to the weight of the poem and only hold it up. If one reads directly from stanza 5 to stanza 13, missing out the intervening stanzas, one has no sense that anything is lost and the transition is more easy than it is as the poem stands. But once over that passage and into stanza 13 one is led through a series of visual images of Zante and of nature, which are direct, fresh, daring and beautiful. The classicism here is not dead; it is alive with the stamp of experience: Nereids still do haunt the waters; while the conceit of stanzas 15 to 17, with the image of the Ionian breeze and wave caressing the body and breasts of Cytherea before caressing the girls of Zante, is one of a fine sensuousness. Indeed the whole passage has a delight and a spontaneity which is surprising, particularly within the convention in which Kalvos wrote.

If, however, we turn from this straightforward lyrical utterance to the last of Kalvos' twenty odes—and, it must be remembered, only two years separated the publication of the first and the last ode—quite another state of affairs presents itself. The poem is as follows:

The Altar of the Fatherland

Hurry, brothers, hurry,
eager, courageous souls;
around the fatherland's
altar shining
hurry always.

Let disunity cease,
disunity which throws the nations,
blindly, beneath the harshest
claws of sleepless
treacherous tyrants.

Hurry here; in concord
let us weave the dance,
each one offering
splendid precious sacrifice
to the fatherland.

Here let us readily
purify our passions;
let us seize arms
only to wound
the Mussulman's breast.

24

Let us pour here
all our wealth; while
we hold the naked sword,
laurel's honoured leaves
suffice us.

And then, when we have shattered
the most hated yoke,
freedom again will give us
other rewards, not
uncertain riches.

Here, friends, let us forsake
pleasure and rest;
a hard stone is the mattress
and poison the bread
of slavery.

Here, as votive offerings,
close beside the altar,
brethren, our children,
loved ones and the elders
now let us leave.

Whatever our heart
most precious holds, it is not fit
for men who cower
before the senseless
barbarian sceptre.

Nor is life fit.
Hurry, brothers, hurry.
In measure let us dance,
in measure let us die
for the fatherland.

There is no need to question Kalvos' sincerity in writing
this poem. No doubt he felt that his country was in danger
because of her internal disunion. No doubt he desired his
fellow-countrymen to sacrifice all private interest and pursuit for the sake of their nation's freedom. No doubt he felt

that without such freedom nothing else had much value. What is of concern here is not Kalvos' sincerity, but whether this is or is not poetry; and the answer is that, even allowing for the gross inadequacy of the translation, it is not. It does not in fact contain a single line that can be called poetry. There is a great deal of mechanical pomp, verbalizing and gesture, but no poetry. It is not simply that Kalvos was trying to make poetry from elements out of which it cannot be made. There is no reason in itself why a poet should not take part in the political events of his times and voice the ideals and hatreds of local faction and party programme, and yet in spite of this still make poetry. Many poets have indeed enriched their work precisely through such participation in contemporary events, Dante and Yeats not being the least among them. But in Kalvos' case not only is the poetry not enriched, it is effectively stifled altogether.

At this point, it will help us to understand the startling lapse of quality between Kalvos' first and his last ode and to sift the pure from the dross in his poetry if a few words are said about an English poet who at first sight may appear to have little in common with the Greek poet. Thomas Gray's position in English poetry is somewhere between that of Pope and Johnson on the one hand, and Keats and Wordsworth on the other. If this position is looked at from a broader point of view, one can say that Gray marks a transition between two periods. In the first everything in the universe was regarded as fixed, established and in order; and the main concern of the poet was with the design of his poem. In the second everything was felt to be in movement, flowing, in growth, without break between one event and the next, organic; and the poet was concerned above all with the continuity and growth of his poem, with its organic development. In the former period, the poet tended to see in terms of a series of static, well-designed pictures, linked by artfully constructed transitions. The poet's great problem in fact was how to present, without losing coherence, a series of scenes, all contemporary, all co-existing, in the successive form which a poem demands. There was very little sense of

26

organic growth within the poem. On the contrary, the actual order of scenes within the poem often seems arbitrary and even irrelevant: the order might quite well be changed without seriously disturbing the poem. The eighteenth century of Pope and Johnson saw in terms of separate pictures, not in terms of movement; and in pictures they saw design, not a reflection of the soul's rhythm. Hence the comparative lack of interest in narrative in this period. In the latter period—that of Keats and Wordsworth—poets began to see all things as continuity, as imperceptible growth, without a transition from one scene to the next. Coleridge could say 'Landscape is music' and could talk of a 'streamy nature'. The change is one from an almost mechanical vision of things to an organic, even to a biological vision: one recalls Goethe's words about producing 'not only something effective . . . but, as a rival of nature . . . something spiritually organic'. Or, from another point of view, important for our theme, it is a change from an attitude which gives to the rational consciousness the major part in the act of creation to one in which a more emotional and irrational element plays a dominant rôle.

Here lies the crux of the difference between the eighteenth century and the Romantic epoch which succeeded it. The qualities which commanded the admiration of the eighteenth-century world—balance, design, harmony—were qualities of the reason. The order and enlightenment respected were a rational order and enlightenment. The deliberate imposition of a chosen form, derived preferably from a classical model, on matter—a purely rational act—was the process whereby a work of art might be achieved. As a result, the emotional and irrational elements of man's nature tended to be suppressed and kept underground. But, since they are a part of life itself, they could not be extinguished. They smouldered on, in deep and swelling ferment, behind the formal neo-classic façade which too often the eighteenth-century vision mistook for the whole of reality, or at least for the whole of reality with which civilized man need concern himself. As far as the poetry of the eighteenth century goes, the vast world of man's emotional and irrational nature was held in check. Or it was nearly held in check. For now and then images from its depths do rise and force their way through to the surface—images of the night, the moon, death, the dark sea, cemeteries—provoking anxiety and a sense of guilt and giving warning to those who had ears to hear of the great upheavals which at the end of the century were to break through and destroy overnight the barriers of reason and order: the upheavals of the French Revolution and of the Romantic poets. One of the eighteenth-century poets who felt this anxiety and had intimations of the turbulent darkness which lay biding its time but growing with the inevitability of the fertilized seed beneath the surface of life and who sensed behind the static vision of the eighteenth century the clamour of new forces rising from within, was Gray.

The poetry of Gray, like the poetry of Kalvos, has a split personality. It stands on that point of rift when the formal, fixed, designing neo-classic convention of the eighteenth-century poetic consciousness, with its series of static, isolated pictures leading up to an appropriate moral tag, begins to give way to a less regular, more sombre awareness. A poem of Gray's such as 'Ode on the Spring' is an example of the neo-classic convention at its best:

> Lo! where the rosy-bosomed Hours,
>   Fair Venus' train, appear,
> Disclose the long-expecting flowers,
>   And wake the purple year.
> The Attic warbler pours her throat,
> Responsive to the cuckoo's note,
>   The untaught harmony of spring;
> While, whispering pleasure as they fly,
> Cool Zephyrs thro' the clear blue sky
>   Their gathered fragrance fling.

Here the lyric impulse is not so direct or so fresh as it is in Kalvos' 'The Patriot': it is more involved with a decorative artificiality, with a conventional neo-classicism; but it is strong enough to carry the poem through with grace and liveliness to the neat finish: 'We frolic, while 'tis May.' But,

28

charming though this kind of writing may be, what a change
and deepening of atmosphere there is if we turn to the 'Elegy
Written in a Country Churchyard':

> Now fades the glimmering landscape on the sight,
>   And all the air a solemn stillness holds,
> Save where the beetle wheels his droning flight,
>   And drowsy tinklings lull the distant folds;
>
> Save that from yonder ivy-mantled tower
>   The moping owl does to the moon complain
> Of such as, wandering near her secret bower,
>   Molest her ancient solitary reign.

What a change in moral climate there is between such pretty
apophthegms as 'Nor all, that glitters, gold' or 'Where
ignorance is bliss 'Tis folly to be wise' and the following lines
from the 'Elegy':

> . . . their crimes confirmed;
> Forbad to wade through slaughter to a throne,
> And shut the gates of mercy on mankind,
>
> The struggling pangs of conscious truth to hide . . .

It is not merely that the poet has changed his mood: it is that
a whole new field of awareness has come into view, a whole
new area of feeling and responsibility, something not
included in the neo-classicism of 'Ode on the Spring': a
warning of darker pains and of deeper misgivings than the
too often too self-satisfied, too complacent and impersonal
mind of the eighteenth century recognized. In Gray's 'Elegy'
there is a tone of doubt and bewilderment heard seldom in
the poetry of the eighteenth century. A small rift has opened
through which is to pour in time the full flood of that sub-
conscious and irrational world which the eighteenth century,
with its growing confidence in man's perfectibility in and
through a properly organized society, its growing belief in
the progress of history towards a civilized and rational
future, and to that end its avoidance of the more torturing
problems of man's inner and intimate existence, had tended

29

to suppress or at least had tried to keep at arm's length.

Gray himself—so far as his poetry is concerned—did not look again into that world after he had finished the 'Elegy'. A year or two later he was back on the more familiar, less threatening ground of:

Awake, Aeolian lyre, awake
And give to rapture all thy trembling strings.
From Helicon's harmonious springs
A thousand rills their mazy progress take . . .

('The Progress of Poetry')

He 'shut the gates of mercy', if not on mankind, at least on those sources from which mankind draws a most fecund, though also a most disturbing sustenance.

In the light of these few remarks on Gray's position in English poetry and on that eighteenth-century ethos in which it was produced, some of the difficulties in approaching Kalvos' poetry may become less obstinate. Kalvos learnt his art within the framework of a poetical convention very similar to that within which Gray wrote. That this should have been the case in spite of the fifty years or so between the youth of one poet and that of the other, can be accounted for by the fact that the Ionian Isles were far removed from the centres of the intellectual life of Europe; that what was being taught in one generation in London or Paris would not affect the educational climate of Zante until the next. Especially is this so where the last half of the eighteenth century is concerned: the changes during this period at the centres of Europe's intellectual life were so rapid that the kind of atmosphere within which Blake wrote his prophetic books could exist at the same time and in the same country as the kind of atmosphere within which Jane Austen wrote her novels. It is not surprising then that Kalvos' conscious tastes and values should have been formed by a convention similar to that which affected Gray—tastes and values which belonged to a world already disrupted in many parts of Europe. And not only was this so where Kalvos' Zakynthian education was concerned; it was so also where his Italian

30

education and, what is more important, where the influence of Foscolo were concerned. Foscolo's tastes and values were still largely those of the neo-classic 'enlightened' eighteenth century. Latin and Greek works were still the great models to which the poet must look. He must try to use their forms, their themes, their imagery and syntax; he must, like them, seek to inculcate moral and civic virtue. 'Converse night and day . . . with the great ones of antiquity,' Foscolo writes in a letter to Kalvos[5]; 'refine your mind', 'establish your judgment', 'nourish soundly your spirit' 'with persistent and burning study of Latin and Greek authors.' It need hardly be pointed out that the eighteenth-century appreciation of the classics was a very one-sided appreciation. In fact, what the eighteenth century saw in ancient poetry was a reflection of the values of its own 'natural philosophy', with its conception of a fixed, ordered, established universe. Its poets sought to reproduce these values in their own poetry. Kalvos inherited their ambition.

Unfortunately—and here we come to what is important for our understanding of Kalvos' situation—this external convention relating to poetry and poetics no longer corresponded to what was seeking expression in Kalvos' inner world. There was, that is to say, a fundamental dislocation between the means of expression and what had to be expressed; or, to put it in terms used when speaking of Gray's poetry, there was a fundamental dislocation between Kalvos' conscious and subconscious worlds. For Kalvos, like Gray and, as we shall see, even more than Gray, possessed doubts and longings and anxieties and was tormented by misgivings incompatible with the balanced, ordered eighteenth-century ethos. He was aware of stresses and tensions, forces and feelings which the eighteenth century—I use the term 'eighteenth century' on these occasions as synonymous with that intellectual outlook already described—had kept at arm's length. Where the eighteenth century had seen civilization and security, he was beginning to see death and destruction; where the eighteenth century had seen taste and wisdom, he was beginning to see artificiality and shallow pomposity. In other words, the climate of Kalvos' inner world was closer to that of the Romantic poets than it was to that of the eighteenth-century poets in whose idiom and according to whose values he was trying to write his poetry.

It is not difficult, at least from an external point of view, to show how this dichotomy may well have arisen. Kalvos spent the first years of his life on his island, Zante. It is easy to imagine what an impression that island and that period of his life made upon his young mind. To begin with, there was the sheer physical beauty of the island's natural scenery, and the delight of so many aspects of its life. Witnesses enough are to be found to testify to this beauty, travellers who, generally speaking, are without the sensibility of a poet. Henry Holland, who visited the island but a few years after the poet had left it, is typical. After describing his arrival at Zante, when the 'fragrant odour' from its plants and flowers was wafted across the sea to him and was 'distinctly perceptible even three miles from the land', he goes on to speak of 'its natural beauties sufficient to awaken all the attention of the stranger' and of the festival of All Saints' Day 'celebrated among the olive-groves near the city; where half the inhabitants of the place were assembled in their best dresses; some were walking, some dancing, others playing on the guitar, or forming a part in the religious processions; and various groups dining under the shade of the olive trees, according to the usage of the day.'[6] These Zakynthian years of Kalvos' childhood were associated, too, with the presence of his mother. Only one of Kalvos' poems presents a definite figure, and that figure is his mother. Moreover, this is also the only poem which has a specific and personal religious content. The beauty of the Zakynthian landscape, the figure of his mother and his religious sense must have been closely inter-related in the poet's consciousness.

At about the age of ten, however, this idyllic life of love, tenderness, festival and natural beauty was suddenly swept away from beneath his feet. He left his island. He left his mother. In the difficult times of his life which followed, Kalvos must have looked back to that period as one of blessedness. His island and his life there, transfigured as it was by absence and nostalgia, must have appeared to him as something ideal, without struggle, bitterness or disruption: a Garden of Eden where, as he says in one of his poems, 'earth was paradise and life one'. It must in fact have corresponded to that vision of the landscape of childhood so vividly described by Traherne; a landscape in which, Traherne writes, 'I knew no childish proprieties, nor bounds nor divisions; but all the proprieties were mine, all treasures and the possessors of them.'[7] As we shall see, in Kalvos' poetry we come again and again across scenes and descriptions of an idyllic life such as that which Traherne describes; and suddenly across these scenes and descriptions fall the shades of the prison-house of proprieties and bounds and divisions, and scenes and descriptions of violence or wilderness or destruction take their place.

Here, then, is a source of Kalvos' essentially romantic temperament: his childhood and youth and the influences dominant in them and his subsequent parting from them. But this quite instinctive and personal romanticism, this longing and nostalgia for an early life and for the feelings and ways associated with it, may in Kalvos' case have received support and, in a sense, justification, from two more literary sources. The first of these was his reading of various pre-Romantic poets and in particular of English 'sepulchral' poets like Parnell, Young or Blair, or even Gray himself, or of melancholy and nostalgic writers like Ossian. Few words need be said about this influence, since it was more an external one than one which corresponded to any deep inner affinity; that is to say, while these poets may have suggested to Kalvos a certain landscape of images—and this applies, as we shall see later, particularly in the case of one poem, Kalvos' ode 'To Death'—the use to which Kalvos put this landscape and what he wanted to express through it were markedly different. The English sepulchral poets, for instance, were not first of all interested in what one might call metaphysical themes, themes of heaven and hell and purgatory; still less were they concerned, as Foscolo was in his famous sepulchral poem 'I Sepolchri', to throw into relief the value and dignity of man in his life. They sought to describe as directly as possible physical corruption and the odours of the tomb, the change from the state of physical well-being to that of bodily dissolution, from worldly pomp to the solemn banquet of worms:

> Methinks I see thee with thy head low laid,
> While surfeited upon thy damask cheek
> The high-fed worm, in lazy volumes rolled,
> Riots unscared. . .

writes Robert Blair; and Thomas Parnell adds the comforting moral reflection to which this contemplation of bones, epitaphs, marble pillars, weeping angels and the charnel house is meant to give rise—that of the virtuous man's undoubted salvation after death:

> Death's but a path that must be trod,
> If man would ever pass to God;
> A port of calms, a state of ease
> From the rough rage of swelling seas.

The true significance of that death and resurrection which lies at the heart of all important spiritual life, and which signifies man's transcendence of his own individuality and his participation in the energies and perceptions of a higher state of existence, has been lost; and the domesticated, emasculated 'religious' consciousness is now focused on a purely natural death leading with prosaic certainty to a purely 'natural' resurrection. Such an attitude does not have a place in Kalvos' world; as we shall see, he still retained some awareness of a less superficial outlook. But there is no doubt that his reading of these poets did sharpen his awareness of his own world and did also provide him with certain images important for his poetry.

The second of these two literary sources which may have lent support to Kalvos' instinctive romanticism is the work of Rousseau. We have seen that when Kalvos was living at Florence in the years after 1813 he gave special place in his studies to Rousseau. He may well have felt in Rousseau's ideas echoes of his own feelings; he may have felt that these feelings were given, as it were, a moral dignity by being so close to those voiced by so famous a man. 'Give us back ignorance, innocence and poverty, which alone can make us happy . . .' wrote Rousseau in his *Discourse on the Arts and Sciences*. He did not mean by this the ignorance, innocence and poverty of man in society; he meant those of pre-social man, of the unspoiled child of nature. In the primitive state of nature, men lived 'free, healthy, honest and happy lives'. Man is naturally good. He is born free and everywhere he is in chains. Crafty and powerful men have broken down and disrupted the state of nature; they have founded a society 'which irretrievably destroyed natural liberty, eternally fixed the law of property and inequality, converted clever usurpation into unalterable right and, for the advantage of a few ambitious individuals, subjected all mankind to perpetual labour, slavery and wretchedness.' For this there was but one cure: to get back as closely as possible and as soon as possible to that original state of nature and to follow nature's laws. Thus *Émile* is a plea for naturalism in education, the *New Héloise* for naturalism in morals. Much of this must have sounded poignantly true to Kalvos, for his own experience must have seemed to bear direct and painful witness to it. When had he been happy but in that pre-social age of youth, surrounded by the beauties of land, sea and sky, living a carefree life of natural and unknowing innocence under the protective care of his mother? And he had been deprived of that happiness by man-made proprieties, bounds and divisions, by artificial conventions and formulas. The Golden Age, the Earthly Paradise, had been broken and disfigured by an alien world; it had been usurped and blotted out.

Nor was this all. Did not in fact the actual state of contemporary Greece as a whole, quite apart from his own sentiment, bear living witness to this same process of the destruction of natural innocence and of gradual enslavement? For there, in Greece (though this Greece may never have existed anywhere but in the dream-world of a totally unreal past)—there, in Greece, men had lived innocent and unspoiled lives until the perverted ambitions of foreign conquerors had 'irretrievably destroyed natural liberty' and had set everyone in chains. In this way, from a purely personal and subjective romanticism Kalvos could elaborate a politico-religious philosophy with which he could integrate his neo-classic vision of ancient Greece and by means of which he could fulfil the eighteenth-century conception of the poet as a public figure who through his poetry could teach and inculcate a social morality and exhort his fellowmen to action. That is to say, he could respectably conventionalize what was, from the point of view of those eighteenth-century values to which he consciously subscribed, a thoroughly disreputable romanticism.

Thus then, by way of this introduction, we reach a better understanding of Kalvos' own personal situation and so perhaps a critical vantage-point from which we are able to appreciate his poetry. On the one hand, there is the Kalvos who consciously seeks to live up to the eighteenth-century conception of the poet, to reflect in his poetry its approved social and moral lessons, and to do all this by means of its poetic convention based on what was regarded as the canons of classical art. This is the external Kalvos, the teacher who through his work is to help society towards its glorious, enlightened and liberated future: the impersonal public figure with a conscious historical rôle, even a maker of history. On the other hand, behind the gestures and the verbalism, the posturing and the moral exhortation, the rigid convention and the pedantic classicism, is Kalvos the person with all his private grief and anxiety, his great longings and sudden insights, his loneliness and despair; with all that submerged world of the exile who remembers with pain his vanished country and his mother's vanished tenderness, and whose intuitions of an almost unearthly earthly beauty and radiance are shattered by a terrible sense of doom and human loss: the Kalvos outside society, outside history, behind the conscious façade, alone in his world of torturing private experience and of little or no consolation. These two sides of Kalvos' nature

36

were never reconciled and integrated: conscious and sub-conscious never became one, as they must if an artist is to develop beyond a certain point. Given the relatively super-ficial values of the eighteenth century which dominated the poet's consciousness, they could not become one; or, to put it the other way round, they could only have become one if the poet had been able to surrender those values for an understanding of life that would have made possible the inte-gration he lacked on a higher level; and this, as we shall see, he was unable to do, just as it was also something that Gray had been unable to do. And as these two sides of Kalvos' nature remained separate and antagonistic in his life, so they remained separate and antagonistic in his poetry; and through their ill-fated division his whole poetic life was, it seems, destroyed.

We can now turn back to Kalvos' own poetry, to trace the phases through which it passed as the living, responsive human voice is slowly stifled beneath the conventional mask and as the freshness of the greater part of 'The Patriot' gives place more and more to the verbiage of 'The Altar of the Fatherland'. First there is the lyric, exciting dawn, when images of daring catch the note of untroubled happiness in an earthly paradise, in a world free from proprieties, bounds and divisions: the golden age of man's youth in a landscape of pristine beauty, in an idealized state of nature and of primitive innocence similar to that of Homer's Ethiopia whose blameless inhabitants lived feasting in joy and were beloved by the gods:

> Now dawn opens the flowers
> on earth's cool breast,
> and now appear
> the works of industrious men.
>
> The scented lips of day
> kiss
> the world's rested forehead;
> dreams, darkness,

sleep, silence vanish, and again
flocks and lyres
fill the fields with sound,
fill sea and air and all the cities. . . .
                                    ('The Ocean')

Or:

Beautifully, sweetly, you appear,
O golden-lashed
daughter of the Sun,
gladly, day, you come forth.

Freeman or slave,
what does it matter—
only let man live,
for earth is Paradise and life one.

Come, while the scented fingers
of Aphrodite
flutter the strings, and the tender
guitar charms the earth;

hasten, you carefree
crowd of people: seize,
young men and girls,
the big delicious jar of Bessareos.

With Sidonian shirt
and gold-laced sandals,
dancing sing
the Lesbian mode or other song.

Enough of drinking now,
enough of song and dance;
if each delight has measure,
let us turn to a fresh joy.

Come here under the thick-leaved
cool cedars:
let us rest our body, let us have

           flowers as mattress. . . .
                       ('To Psara')

Or again:

           . . . O home of the Zephyrs,
           when elsewhere the sun's
           rays scorch the mountains
           or winter night cuts the springs,

           then your breast flowers,
           your skies shine,
           and your fruit-bearing
           trees always are laden.

           As, before night falls,
           the sweet star of Aphrodite
           alone shines out
           in the blue air;

           as the proud myrtle,
           heavy with flowers and dew,
           gleams when the gold-girdled
           dawn greets her:

           so the ship, beating
           the Icarian wave, sees
           you among the islands
           splendid and towering, and rejoices. . . .
                       ('To Samos')

All this corresponds to a state of primordial innocence: a kind of childhood state before consciousness is awakened and divides life into antinomies; and this state is conveyed in a series of separate and static images which succeed one another with little organic link but which often have a vivid sensuousness and beauty.

Then consciousness and thought awaken and disrupt the harmony of life by their questionings and probings. The mind begins to impose its own laws and divisions over the lyric, idyllic and idealized landscape of childhood innocence;

shades of the prison-house begin to fall. In Kalvos' personal life we can find a counterpart for this in his leaving Zante, his mother and his childhood to face an unknown, lonely and uprooted world; or, from a deeper mythological point of view, we can see it as that phase in human life which we express as the sunset or the overthrow of the gods: as man's loss of paradisaical innocence and his waking to a world of mind-forged manacles, moral law, and physical bondage. But just as Kalvos gave his instinctive feeling for and insight into childhood innocence and natural beauty a poetic and political respectability by expressing them in terms of an idealized Arcadian landscape, so now he conventionalized his sense of loss, rupture, spoliation and imprisonment by projecting it in terms of political indignation at the over-running of Greece by the Turks and at the spectacle of his country under a foreign yoke. Nevertheless, it is the pathos of genuine experience which sounds in such lines as the following, an experience we can easily identify and which must have been one of genuine pain for Kalvos:

> . . . If before nightfall the sea
> separates the bold
> sailor from his island,
>
> with bitter soul
> he stands at the prow
> gazing at the stillness and the twilight
> which hovers above the water.
>
> He sees the beloved
> mountains and fields
> of his dear country
> red still from the sun.
>
> But already in the dark
> bowl of the West
> sinks the last ray
> of the shining king of the air.

40

And the island cliffs
change and darken, as the young
face of an orphan
wet with clouds of distress . . .
        ('To the British Muse')

  With this description of man's parting from his land of innocence and of his entering the world of darkness and estrangement, go other images of loss:

Smoke saddens the blue
distance of the sky, as
in the mist of death
a smile chokes a child. . . .
        ('To Chios')

Or:

Streams of forgetfulness
spill from the vase and make
everything vanish:
cities, kingdoms, nations are lost.
        ('To the Sacred Company')

Or:

Ah, the hopes of man
dissolve
as the light dreams of a child;
they sink as fine shot
to the sea's fathomless depth.
        ('To the British Muse')

Scenes of desolation, of wilderness, of a paradise deserted replace those of the happy life:

Green, sweet-smelling
isles of the Aegean sea,
happy lands
where joy and peace always dwell:

41

where now are your splendid
girls who had
souls like fire, lips
like cool roses, throats like milk?

In your rich gardens
basil and lilies
flower vainly: alone,
not one hand left to tend them.

Your woods, your ravines
where the hunter's voice used to echo
are silent: only
masterless dogs bark there.

Horses free and unbridled
gallop among the vines
and on them only
rides the breath of the wind.

Fearless, crying, gulls and falcons
descend
from the clouds
down to the shore.

Deep in the sand I see
tracks of living
children and men;
but where are the men, where are the children . . .

('The Volcanoes')

Over this scene of desolation all that is left is the sense of
sorrow:

As the afflicted noonday wind
blows
through the wood of evening
like a human dirge:

so ocean-daughters bear
to the deserted island
the waves
and their lamenting.
('To Chios')

In no poem, however, is this experience of the loss of life
and of total eclipse darkening all man's existence so vividly
expressed as in the ode 'To Death'. This is at the same time
an ode to the poet's mother. Her death is the symbol of this
overwhelming loss, just as her life is the symbol of the state
of innocence and blessedness. She thus takes on an aspect
which is more than merely autobiographical. She becomes in
some sense the Mother: she whose arms are always open to
the child when he flies from the bitter rods and endless tor-
ments of the world; she in whom man seeks the dim, comforting memory of that warmth and peace of his life before
the waking of consciousness, of the milk-like consolation
which soothes his dreams of innocence; whose only law is
love and whose only sentence forgiveness; who is the ground
of life itself and of its fruitfulness, and so is linked intimately
with that inner world of man from which his own life and
fruitfulness rise. She stands in fact for all that is opposite to
the world of rational consciousness, the world of laws, pres-
criptions, moral codes and political programmes, 'enlightenment' and culture; opposite, one might add, to those values
and standards of the eighteenth-century world by which
Kalvos was increasingly dominated. Hence, more than any
other, this is a key poem in Kalvos' work, for it issues from
the heart of his own personal situation as well as from the
heart of a perennial human situation. The setting of the
poem is one which Kalvos may well have 'borrowed' from
the sepulchral poets—that of a graveyard at night, with its
tombs and cold moons and phantoms:

To Death

Here in this church,
building of the first Christians,
how came I,
kneeling?

43

Huge wings of midnight,
silent, black, frozen,
cover the earth.

Quiet here: relics
of the saints sleep;
quite quiet: do not disturb
the sacred rest of the dead.

I hear the rushing of the wind's fury;
madly it beats; windows
of the church open,
torn to pieces.

From the sky
where black-winged clouds sail
the moon
throws her cold silver;

and she lights a chill
white silent tombstone:
spent censers, spent candles, funeral cakes
cover the grave.

O God in Heaven, what stirs?
What possesses me? My hair
stands on end and my breath stops.

See, the tomb shakes!
See, from the crack rises
a white vapour
and stands before me.

It thickens, takes
a human form.
Who are you? Tell me. Creature
or ghost of my troubled mind?

Or are you someone
who dwells in the tomb?
You smile? From Heaven
or from Hell—tell me whence you come?

44

The phantom is the poet's mother. She now addresses her
son, comparing her release with mortal affliction as she
answers his last question:

'Do not ask. Do not search out
the inexpressible
mystery of death. You behold
the breast that suckled you before you.

O my child, my child,
my tender loved one,
our fates are separate, and
vainly you seek to clasp me.

Stop your tears, calm
your heart's anguish;
if in unhoped-for joy you weep because you see me,

rejoice, rather, and be glad;
if you complain because I left the sun,
console yourself.

What do you lament? Unknown
to you is my soul's state;
and in the grave my body rests from labour.

Yes, life is unsupportable labour;
hopes and fears,
joys and delights of the world
torment you.

Here we the dead enjoy
everlasting peace, a sleep
fearless, sorrowless,
without dream.

You, cowards, tremble,
hearing the name
of inescapable death.

One only is the road
and leads
to the tomb; indomitable fate
compels the living there.

My son, alive you knew me:
the sun spider-like revolving
wound me
ceaselessly with light and death.

The spirit that gave me life
was God's breath
and to God has returned:
my body was earth, and fell here to the grave.

But the light of the moon
fades, and I must leave you.
I shall see you again
when life forsakes you, and only then.

Go, and my blessing with you.
I say no more. What remains
I shall disclose later.
Farewell, my child, farewell. . .'

The vision vanishes, leaving the poet 'in thick darkness'. He now laments her absence and proclaims his intention to cross over the abyss which separates them—a 'crossing over' that represents a triumph over death and death's laws:

O voice, O mother,
consolation of my childhood,
eyes which shed on me sweet tears:

and you, mouth that I kissed
so many times, with such
warm love, how many
boundless abysses divide us?

Ah, let them be boundless,
and more than boundless,

46

intrepidly I shall cross them,
seeking you.

Now my lips can kiss
the knees of death,
now can I crown his skull.

Where are the roses? Fetch
the fadeless wreaths and the lyre.
Sing.
The terrible enemy has become a friend.

Can he who embraced frail woman
put fear
into the heart of man?

Who is in danger?
Now that I face death with courage
I hold
the anchor of salvation.

As the eagle flies from mountain to mountain,
so I scale
the difficult cliffs of virtue.

We have called this a key poem from two points of view.
First, because it issues from the heart of Kalvos' own
personal situation, and second, because it reveals a perennial
human situation and one which became particularly acute
towards the end of the eighteenth century. In fact, the 'split'
we have recognized in Kalvos' personality and which is
reflected in his poetry is also that which threatened to destroy
and in the end did destroy the balanced intellectual ethos of
the eighteenth century. The 'split' in both cases resulted from
an inability to reconcile and integrate the rational and
irrational elements of human life on a higher level, on a level
of understanding that transcends the purely rational level. By
and large the eighteenth century had suppressed or had
attempted to suppress what did not conform to the single
vision of the mind; it had tended to think that what was true

must be rational and that to believe in what was not rational was a sign of superstition, or marked a stage in human development which man must surpass. Rational truth was what it most valued, not supra-rational truth. In his ode 'To Death', Kalvos steps out of the closed world of the eighteenth century and reveals the depths beyond. This comes about by a strange but crucial logic. That state of paradisaical pre-conscious innocence from which life had 'fallen' was, for reasons we have seen, associated for Kalvos with his mother; his mother symbolized this state for him. But now this mother was dead and in the kingdom of death — buried, one might say, in the deepest recesses of the poet's memory. Thus, by that strange logic of which we have spoken, that lost paradisaical state, symbolized by the mother, now itself exists in the kingdom of death, in the unexplored depths of the human memory. It follows that the only way of recovering it is by going beyond the limits of the conscious daylight world and by penetrating into and resuscitating those inner depths of memory:

> . . . how many
> boundless abysses divide us?

> Ah, let them be boundless,
> and more than boundless,
> intrepidly I shall cross them
> seeking you.

Man's life is a ceaseless revolving between light and death. Somewhere beyond the gulf which opens at the frontiers of the daylight world of rational consciousness is the other world. To realize this other world so that its vitalities and understandings penetrate and enrich his ordinary mortal life, man must cross over this gulf. He must visit death's kingdom. This is the recognition which Kalvos' 'To Death' expresses.

But what happens? Does Kalvos in fact seek to live out this recognition? On the contrary, like Gray he shuts the gates, puts on the mask, postures, talks of scaling cliffs of virtue

48

or, in another poem, of playing the lyre at the edge of the open tomb. He does not in fact (at least as far as we can judge from his poetry) realize the full significance of that metaphysical death, if one may call it that, which lies at the heart of all important spiritual experience and which is the prelude to any real life. He remains on this side of it. He does not cross the gulf which divides him from that fuller state of existence of which he is aware. George Seferis, in a critical study of Kalvos' work, has compared Kalvos with Hamlet: 'The Prince of Denmark wishes to kill the murderer of his father, and he kills, behind the screen, Polonius. What has happened to him? He explains and talks when he should be acting. The same thing happens sometimes to Kalvos: he talks, he does not act. Poetry is also an action . . .'[8]

This is a just assessment. Kalvos had a sense of human destiny which went beyond that of the eighteenth century within whose conventions he wrote and to a large extent lived. But instead of remaining true to this sense and realizing that destiny and the vision of life that went with it, he dressed both up in a mass of moral, literary and political verbiage borrowed from contemporary fashion, and in the end he smothered them altogether. He was unwilling or unable to face the reality of which he was aware. He sacrificed the private being, to whom the poet must always remain faithful, to the impersonal public and conventional figure of the poet. His decision to go to Greece to '*exposer un coeur de plus au feu de Musulmans*' was in fact simply one further rhetorical gesture with which he sought to avoid what for him would have meant real action: an attempt to heal the breach in his divided nature. Such action would have meant for him a vital re-orientation. It is a big step from that optimism which leads man to think he can find perfectibility and happiness in and through a properly organized society and which pre-supposes therefore man's natural goodness—it is a big step from this optimism to a view which sees life in society and nature as tragic conflict and struggle in which man's worst enemy is himself. Kalvos, it seems, was not able to make that step. He clung to his public optimism in spite of his inner knowledge of a world beyond such optimism. As a result, his gesture of self-sacrifice for the sake of his country, being but a gesture, crumbled at the first touch of reality. As we have seen, Kalvos left Greece for Corfu a few days after his arrival at Navplia and, so far as his poetry is concerned, the rest is silence.

General Makriyannis: The Portrait of a Greek

THE GREEK WAR OF INDEPENDENCE broke out in 1821. During the years of fighting which followed, may men achieved a renown which has since become legendary—men like Kolokotronis, Mavromikhailis, Kanaris or Androutsos. Another of the heroic figures of this war is General Makriyannis. When the war was over, Makriyannis was appointed General Director of the Executive power of the Peloponnese and Sparta, with his headquarters at Argos. There, as he puts it in his own words,

> so as not to waste time in cafés and such like which I am not used to—(I knew little writing, for I had not gone to a master for reasons which I shall explain, not having the means)—I asked one friend and another to teach me something more here in Argos, where I sit inactive. When therefore I had spent one or two months learning what letters you see, I conceived the idea of writing my life, what I did in my childhood and what I did in the community, when I came of age, and what I did for my country, when I entered into the mystery of the Society* for the struggle for our freedom and what I saw and know of what happened in the Struggle. . .

And immediately Makriyannis set to work and carried out his idea. He went further. He continued to write of events and of his part in them until late on his life—until, in fact, he was physically prevented from continuing. These memoirs of General Makriyannis, which for many years were lost and were only published in 1907, form a unique historical

---

*The *Philiki Etairia*, a secret society established at Odessa in 1814 to promote the movement for liberation from the Turks among the Greek people.

document.[1] They also give us the portrait of a man of remarkable rarity.

Makriyannis was born in the early 1790s. He recounts the circumstances of his birth at the beginning of his memoirs:

> The place of my birth is outside Lidoriki—(in Roumeli)—, a village of Lidoriki called Avoriti—three hours' distance from Lidoriki is the other village, five cottages. My parents were very poor and this poverty came from the pillaging of the occupying Turks and of the Albanians of Ali Pasha. Large-familied my parents and poor, and when I was still in my mother's womb, she went one day into the forest for wood. Loading the wood on to her shoulder, laden for the road, in the wilderness, the pains seized her and she gave birth to me; alone and exhausted the poor woman was in danger of her life and I also. She completed the birth and tidied herself up, she loaded herself with some wood and put grass on top of the wood and on top put me, and she went into the village. In a little time three murders took place in our house and my father was killed. The Turks of Ali Pasha wanted to make slaves of us. Then by night all the family and all our brethren rose up and fled to Livadia to live there. They had to cross a bridge of Lidoriki called the Narrow Bridge: the river couldn't be crossed in another place. There the Turks guarded to seize them as they crossed, and eighteen days they wandered in the woods and all ate wild acorns and I was at the breast and fed on this milk. Unable to bear hunger more, they decided to cross the bridge, and so that I, a small child, should not cry out and all be lost, they decided to throw me into the wood, called the Red Wood, and to go forward to the bridge. Then my mother repented and said to them: 'The crime of the child will be our undoing . . . you cross over and draw off to the other side and stop . . . I take the child and if I am lucky and he doesn't cry, we cross over.' . . . My mother and God saved us.

That was the beginning of Makriyannis' life, a fitting baptism into the world in which he was to live. The next few years were spent wth his mother at Livadia. They were hard, lean years. There was nothing to spare, not even enough to go round. At the age of seven, Makriyannis began to work, to relieve his family of part of the burden. He did not like the work, he tells us:

Since I did many jobs, they wanted me to do menial tasks about the house and to look after the children. That was my death. I didn't want to do that work and my masters and my relations beat me. I rose up and took other children and we went to Thebes. By bad luck my relations came and caught us and took me back to Livadia and to the same master. And for some time I followed the same service. Then to escape from that service, since my honour didn't leave me quiet night or day, I began beating the children on the head with a stick, and even my own mother, and I fled into the rocks. And with that they were fed up and freed me, for in that service I was at the end of my tether.

In 1811, then, Makriyannis moved to Arta, where he worked as an overseer to a man from the same village as his own family. It was there that he began his first trading adventures. In front of the house where he worked was a small square, where the chief men and traders of the town used to come and sit on summer evenings. Makriyannis had to clean the place. He got to know all the people who came there. He managed to raise a loan from them. He bought oats from the villagers, threshed and sold them at a greater price. There was a plague at Arta and a bread shortage. Makriyannis profited by the rise in prices. By 1821, the year of the outbreak of the War of Independence, he had made quite a fortune. It was an important thing. It gave him economic independence during the whole war.

There is one other incident from Makriyannis' childhood which is illuminating. It concerns how he came by his arms as the result of a sacred contract. He was fourteen when he made the contract. It was a feast day, the feast of St John. He went with his master to the feast:

He gave me his gun to hold. I wanted to fire it. It went off. Then he seized me in front of everybody and beat me to death. It wasn't the beating which hurt so much, it was the disgrace in front of everybody. Then all ate and drank and I wept. As I didn't find anyone to tell of my woe to defend me, I thought it right to turn to St John, for in his house this injury and dishonour befell me. I go at night into his church and close the door and begin crying with a loud voice and with obeisances: 'What is

this that has happened to me, am I an ass that they beat me?'
And I beseech him to give me good arms, of silver, and fifteen
purses of money, and I will make him a big silver candle-stick.
With much weeping I made the agreement with the saint.

St John kept to the contract. And when, many years later,
Makriyannis had the money, he made his silver rifle, pistols
and other weapons and the silver candle-stick.

> And armed well and dressed up I took the candle-stick and went
> to my protector and benefactor and true friend, St John, and it
> is still there today—I have my name written on the candle-stick,
> and I made obeisance to him with tears from deep within me, for
> I remembered all the hardships I had tasted . . .

Yet these incidents from Makriyannis' youth are but pre-
ludes to the part he was to play in that great movement which
for years had been slowly maturing among the Greek people.
Here something must be said about the growth and development of this movement in the consciousness of the
Greek people, and in particular in the consciousness of
Makriyannis as representative of that people. For this, however, it is not enough simply to recount the events which led
up to the War of Independence, for these, by themselves,
may be entirely misleading. One must seek behind events
and try to penetrate to that psychological background from
which events, like the visible part of an iceberg, emerge. This
psychological background—or, if you will, feeling for life,
or philosophy of life—is often the product of generations. It
is hard, after a lapse of time, to grasp it. Yet a historian who
does not perceive it writes a history which is little more than a
mass of debris. That is why men like Makriyannis are so
important to the historian. They are the living embodiment
of this feeling; they reveal to us that hidden background of
history which is so often ignored and embody the myth in
which it is expressed. For the original expression of the
psychological background of a people, of their feeling for
life, is myth. Myth is, as it were, the projection of the sub-
conscious aspirations of a people, the way through which a
people becomes conscious of its historical destiny, of its own

latent powers. Every great historical movement has its origin in a myth which provides the model for it, and such a movement may be said to be successful in so far as it realizes that model. Men like Makriyannis did not make the War of Independence. They and the war itself were created by the myth of a free Greece. From one point of view, Makriyannis is a victim, a possessed figure. He is the product of a racial consciousness which has been enshrined in a continuous tradition of myth, legend and poetry. He is as someone appointed for a mission, not appointed by a government or by a state, but by his country's history itself.

This myth of a free Greece, of which the War of Independence represented the historical actualization, was promoted by, and in its turn promoted, a deep sense of patriotism. Readers of Makriyannis' memoirs may be surprised at the frequent occurrence of passages like 'Nothing is greater than one's country' or 'As I love my country I love nothing else. If one comes and tells me that the country will go forward, I consent that he put out my two eyes. For if I am crippled and the country is well, it nourishes me; if the country is sick, ten eyes let me have, a cripple will I be.' They may smile at the reverence with which he regards his country, at his devotion to her, at his insistence that all be sacrificed for her. Patriotism is somewhat debased coinage in our age, and we tend to suspect its motives. That is because we have confused it with a false patriotism, a chauvinism, or an attitude of 'my country right or wrong'—with, in fact, a nationalism. True patriotism has little to do with this nationalism. True patriotism is like a love-affair: it is an expression of Eros. The country is a loved person through whom man seeks contact with what is deepest in his nature; she corresponds to a kind of eternal feminine, Goethe's *Ewig-Weibliche*, and through her he fulfils that longing for self-realization which lies at the roots of every human soul. Perhaps it is only people who remain close to the earth on which they dwell and whose whole emotional sphere is animated by a strong life of earthly origin, in whom this feeling is active. We have so destroyed our roots that few of us nowadays are aware of it. But at a time when there was a people's civilization such as there was in the Greece of Makriyannis, fragments of which we now collect under the name of folk-lore to compensate for our own loss, each man and woman must have experienced this feeling. Certainly at any rate Makriyannis himself did.

This patriotism, as I said, promoted the myth of a free Greece. Indeed, such patriotism made freedom imperative. Where there is a personal and subjective relationship of an individual with his country, any attack on the country must be felt as an attack on that relationship, and so an attack on the individual himself. To soil and to subjugate what has virtually a sacred value for him is to deprive man of his sense of his own dignity and significance. Such deprivation must always be intolerable for those in whom the instinct to live is still vital. It was intolerable for men like Makriyannis.

It is from this point of view that it can be seen how for men like Makriyannis the War of Independence was a religious movement, the fulfilment of a mission. It was not simply a physical matter of expelling the Turks from Greece. It was also a matter of establishing the reign of justice. The Turks had to be fought not only because they were an occupying power, but because they prevented the Greek people from becoming themselves, from possessing the historical existence to which they felt they had the right. As Makriyannis saw it, the Turks had strayed from the road of God; they had overstepped the limits of human behaviour, and those who took upon themselves the responsibility of punishing them for their transgression were no less than divine ministers, scourges of Justice. Time and again, Makriyannis reveals this idea implicitly in his memoirs. 'We will be defeated, we will be defeated', he makes a Turkish Bey cry out at the onset of the war. 'For this war is neither with the Russian, nor with the English, nor with the Frank. We have wronged the Greek and we have deprived him of riches and honour; and his eyes have blackened and he has raised the rifle against us.' And later, after a battle in which the Turks, although they fought bravely, were beaten,

56

Makriyannis comments: 'But injustice, whatever bravery does, is defeated, for the Turks had left the road of God.' In other words, behind the War of Independence as Makriyannis presents it to us in his memoirs, behind history itself as he saw it, lies a dramatic vision of human destiny. This vision sees history not simply as a sequence of events, which is how many professional historians see it, but as the arena in which is played out a vital drama between injustice and justice, crime and the punishment of crime, evil and goodness. Behind the actions on the historical plain, human, heroic and tragic, and giving significance to these actions —giving them their humanity, their heroism and their tragedy—is this vision of divine justice. As in a play by Aeschylus—as, for instance, in the *Agamemnon*—so in the history of the War of Independence as Makriyannis gives it to us, can be discerned the lineaments of a supernatural, symbolic drama where powers that correspond to Hybris and Peitho, to Nemesis and Ate, move in solemn, awe-inspiring majesty. It is this which takes the War as Makriyannis describes it out of the suburb of mere history and places it in the perspective of myth-history, in which events have significance to the degree to which they express aspects of that symbolic drama in which they are involved.

The War of Independence, then, had for Makriyannis the character of a religious movement, with its own mysteries, its own votaries, its own initiation. With what solemnity he regarded it can be gathered from his account of his own initiation into the secret society—the *Philiki Etairia*—formed in Greece at the beginning of the nineteenth century to further the war. In Arta, Makriyannis had a great friend, who loved Makriyannis as one of his own children. This friend had been initiated into the secret society. He was going to initiate Makriyannis, but then changed his mind. This happened several times. Makriyannis felt insulted. He felt his friend considered him unworthy, and he left him and he refused to see him. At last the friend, with tears in his eyes, persuaded Makriyannis to allow him to initiate him. 'I went', continues Makriyannis.

He takes down the icons and makes me swear on them and begins to initiate me. As he continued, then I swore I would not betray it to anyone; but he must give me eight days to think over whether I am worthy of this secret, and if I can serve . . . I left thoughtfully and brought all before me—the killings, the dangers, the struggles—I would suffer them for the freedom of my country and for my religion. I went and said to him: 'I am worthy'. I kissed his hand, I made the vow. I asked him not to reveal to me the signs of the initiation, for I am young and might not resist and anxious for my life might betray the secret and the country be in danger. We agreed about this . . .

The years which followed Makriyannis' initiation were years of war. During the struggle, in which Makriyannis quickly rose to a commanding rank, his life was one long series of battles. He fought at Arta, at Athens, at Navplia, in the Peloponnese—wherever he found the enemy. In these battles, Makriyannis revealed himself to be a born leader, with great tactical sense, physical endurance, and with an extraordinary personal courage. In defence, he took up the attitude of never yielding except through death, and such was the respect in which his command was held that he only had to give an order to defend a position to ensure that it would be defended. In fact, while he was in command he never lost a single battle. The extract which follows comes from Makriyannis' account of his great defence of the Acropolis at Athens in 1826. It illustrates admirably the nature of the warfare in which Makriyannis was engaged and those qualities which made him the leader he was. It also reveals the extraordinary graphic and dramatic power of Makriyannis' writing, a power quite instinctive and unstudied. The siege had been on for a long time. Makriyannis' position was a little outside the walls of the Acropolis—the fort, as it then was; he held the rooms of the Serpetze, that is, the Odeion of Herodes Atticus:

A Christian came and told us secretly that the Turks would move with great strength against my post and would capture the rooms beneath the Serpetze . . . and would enter the fort. For in that place were the mouths of the subterranean tunnels of the

Turks and our own as well. We had also one tunnel prepared against them but we hadn't put any gunpowder in. Then, when we learnt of the movement of the Turks, we hurried Lagoumitzi to go and secure it, to put in the gunpowder. Lagoumitzi said to me: 'The tunnel is beneath the Turks and will resound when I secure it, and the Turks will hear me; and I shall be in danger. If you protect me,' he said to me, 'I enter; otherwise I shan't go in, for I'm in danger.' 'Go and do your job and I'll protect you. And if I die, then you die.' Lagoumitzi went in. I had been sleepless so many nights; night and day we had worked to make trenches; and I had made my rampart also. I went to sleep. The Turks, hearing the hammering of Lagoumitzi, gathered a number of themselves together and made an assault, and came to outside my rampart . . . Then my men engaged with the Turks. I rose suddenly from where I was lying. I stood on the rampart. The Turks shot at me, I shot at them in the mass. They gave me a burst and wounded me in the throat. Then I made a step to come down from the rampart. I fell. The place was narrow; my men were fighting from the outer rampart. They trod on me and went on and (the place was narrow) they crushed me. They saw also the blood, they thought that I was killed. When all had passed and few were left and these were going into the fort, then the Turks would have gone in with them. Katzikostathis was inside; he left his post and fled and went through the door into the fort, into the church; and no one was fighting the Turks. Then I rose half-unconscious and I kept some ten men outside with the knife; I didn't let them go in. And I shut the door which they had open and we started to fight and we fought with pistols. Neither the Turks could fire a rifle, nor us; and we fought for about three hours there. The Turks made a charge, they wounded me again in the head, on the crown. My body was covered with blood. My men sought to take me to go in; then I say to them: 'Brothers, whether we go in or whether we remain outside we are lost, if we do not hold the Turks and free Lagoumitzi' (for the Turks had the mouths of the tunnels and Lagoumitzi at their disposal). I tell them, if we do not hold out and they capture Lagoumitzi, the fort is lost and ourselves with it. But we will hold out. Then the brave Greeks stood like lions . . . The afternoon passing, I shared out the cartridges between the men; other friends joined us. A fresh lot of Turks came also; they fired at us furiously, entered the rooms, took

59

possession of them all and opened the loopholes and fired into the fort. They came at us furiously to take our rampart also . . . I was wounded again very badly in the back of the head; the cloth of the fez went into the bone, to the covering of the mind. I fell as dead. The men dragged me in; then I came to myself. I said to them: 'Leave me to die here, so that living I don't see the Turks overrun my post.' Then the poor Greeks grieved for me; they fought bravely, they drove the Turks from our rampart, and they closed them all in the rooms . . . Then Lagoumitzi escaped and came out to us; he found me in that state. He told me he would stay there, I to stay in the fort for the doctor to bind me up. I said to him: 'Go in. If I die, the fort isn't lost; if you die, it is lost.' Our men held on above the Serpetze and threw burning rags and grass into the rooms. The smoke choked the Turks. Our whole company held their rifles ready. Near evening, the Turks made to come out, our men fired at them in the mass and Turks enough were killed.

But this fighting of the enemy was only one of the fights in which Makriyannis was engaged. He had also to struggle with his own men, with their uncontrollable natures, their lack of discipline, their frequent brutality and their selfishness which threatened the whole purpose of the war. It is perhaps difficult for a modern European quite to realize the nature of the forces with which Makriyannis had to deal. Modern western society, developing under an Aristotelian aegis, has, in its effort to impose form and order upon recalcitrant matter, tended to sacrifice the irrational, chthonic side of man's nature and to establish the reason at the centre of life. No doubt mediaeval Christianity, with its insistence on the diabolic character of so many of man's instincts and of the world's natural manifestations, encouraged this process. But the Renaissance also, which is often supposed to have reinstated nature and the irrational side of life, in fact only strengthened the position of the reason; for what it discovered in nature was a new and fascinating *object*, which gave the illusion that the mind, identified more and more merely with the reason, was the all-powerful and supreme factor of man's life, of all life. Thus the mind-nature dichotomy was accentuated still more until, in the Ages of

Enlightenment which followed the Renaissance, man came to give value to his rational capacities to the exclusion of almost every other part of himself. As a result the irrational, instinctive forces of man's nature have been so suppressed and crippled that it is now a question of whether his whole creative life is not in danger of extinction.

Greece, however—and I refer to the Greece of Makriyannis' time, not of the present day—never had any Middle Ages, as we understand them, or any Renaissance, as we understand it, or an Age of Enlightenment. That elevation of the reason over the rest of life had not taken place. Greece had not gone through that debauchery of rationalism of which the modern western world is the product. Her people had not known that split between mind and instinct, head and heart, and the consequent paralysis of man's emotional life. On the contrary, for a variety of reasons which do not matter here, the Greek people had remained for centuries very close to the earth on which they lived and as a result the irrational, chthonic aspect of their nature was stronger than their capacity for form and order. Their life was founded not on a part of themselves, as is that of the western rationalist, but on the whole of themselves. Their character was much more a direct expression of the forces of nature than the product of any self-conscious training or control. Hence their extreme ego-centredness; hence, from an external point of view, the disorder and in-consequence of their life; hence, too, their spontaneity, naturalness and sincerity: what they did was not the result of premeditation or reflection but simply the breaking forth of the original life-stream itself. This life-stream is neither good nor bad; it has no moral character at all; it is essentially amoral. It is as likely to be destructive as creative, brutal as considerate. It simply *is*, pure energy which in itself has no purpose other than to break forth and whose nature is entirely blind and selfish. That in fact, where Greece is con-cerned, its breaking forth was not always blind and selfish but, as in the case of the War of Independence, was directed towards definite and communal ends, was due to that vitality

61

which enabled the Greek people to project their deepest aspirations in the form of a myth to which the individual could dedicate his life. But this dedication was likely to disappear as soon as its object was attained, and the blindness and selfishness to assert themselves once more. For with the central nerve of his being attached to chthonic, irrational powers, and not to any rational principle or to any principle capable of being rationalized, the Greek was far more at the mercy of uncontrollable, violent impulses than anyone can be who has lost this original earthly contact with the forces of nature.

It was with these forces that Makriyannis had to wrestle in his effort to prevent the war from degenerating into lawlessness and anarchy. He had taken upon himself the responsibility of being a leader and with it the responsibility of keeping some order over his men. Often he had to have recourse to measures which in themselves caused him deep pain. He describes one such occasion in the following passage. Some of his men have looted a village after Makriyannis has promised the inhabitants that nothing will happen to them:

> When those men had looted the village bare and the unfortunate inhabitants had come before me and had wept and I couldn't help them, that was death for me. I took my standard, and some twenty men, whom I had as a squad in my headquarters, and I fled secretly, without those vile soldiers of mine knowing, and we went down to the river. It was in full flood, for it was winter, Christmas; it was dangerous for me and my horse and other strong pack-animals to cross over. When the soldiers learnt that I had fled secretly they followed on close behind me. On the road they came across four Peloponnesians and they seized them and these four Peloponnesians carried half the company one by one on their shoulders across the river (the others had pack-horses and passed over). While they were carrying them across the river, I was there and I had a fire alight with my men and we were eating and I saw all that tyranny they inflicted on those four men, how they maltreated them in the river and how they became black like Arabs from the cold; and how in return for saving them from the river they took the arms

which they had as well; and they left them naked; and they cried like little children; and they shivered with cold. I was very upset on their account and I said that beast is beast but man is worse. When they saw me, they cried out and were full of anger with me and said to me: 'Hearing that you were passing, Makriyannis, who keep your men in such good order, we had confidence and we left our possessions out and we did not hide them away; and you have plundered us naked; and our lives were in danger carrying those men across the river; and they have taken our arms and our clothes and we shiver; and we will die of cold.' I attended the men and I told them to show me who had robbed them. I had decided to kill myself with them. I saddled the horse, I took hold of those with the belongings of the men; I took with me those who were stripped and those who had stripped them, and I went at evening into the village, where I would lodge. I go out and cut good stout sticks and I send out and all the officers come. I said to them: 'I have had most of you many years; have I ever left you unpaid or starving? When as patriots we do our duty, citizens honour us and nourish us with gratitude. . . . When you behaved honourably, I was your leader; now that you take the leadership into your own hands you rob the village when the people wait for us as their brothers, Christians as Christians, you rob them of their belongings, their animals, you take their flocks with you. I am not going to become your shepherd; go and find another leader, or let the villagers come and you give back their belongings and their animals so that they miss nothing; and when the villagers have given acknowledgement, then stay with me. Otherwise, find another leader . . .' Then we sent and the villagers came and took their goods and I received the acknowledgement from them themselves.

Then I take those who had stripped the men in the river, I detail five officers and each holds one man. I beat. I took out my pistols and said: 'Whoever loosens one of those men from those who hold them, or wants to defend them, let him take his arms and we will fight to the death; not men to become pack-horses in the river and to carry other men over on their shoulders and then those men to rob them afterwards for their kindness.' I placed the four men on the ground and they held them lying down. One by one I beat them till blood came from behind. I was worse than they; my hands were shreds; I was many days sick . . .

63

From many points of view, however, the great trial for Makriyannis came only in the years after the war with the problem of how to communicate the need for order not simply to his own men, but to the nation as a whole and, in particular, to those who had its government in their control. He understood that without the corresponding check of form—form as law and good government—the revolutionary ardour and ideals of his compatriots would dissolve into chaos and internal turbulence and into an anarchy in which everyone sought to realize his own interests in complete disregard of the interests of everyone else. If this happened, there would have been no real conquest, no real fulfilment of the purpose of the war itself. 'My country without laws and administration is in danger.' 'What nation without administration and laws is not lost?' Such phrases run like a refrain through Makriyannis' memoirs. The unity which even during the war had been, to say the least, most precarious, might, now that the war was over, disintegrate into a squalid struggle for personal gain. That is always a difficulty with a people who, like the Greeks, seem at their best when most egotistical. While a threat to individual existence affects a sufficient number of individuals, corporate action performs feats of incredible heroism, the most insurmountable obstacles are surmounted. But once the threat is gone, the essential egoism again asserts itself, and the apparent collectivism is seen to have been simply a body of isolated individuals whose energies happened to have worked at the same time in the same direction, but in whom the sense of collectiveness was momentary and in no way binding. This contradiction seems ever-present in Greek history—the conflict of Apollo and Dionysos. It accounts for the great number of exceptional achievements performed by the Greek people, for the energy is never suffocated or rationalized away and is always likely to break out; it also accounts for the great instability of life, for those things which provide stability—institutions, laws, organizations, all of which require for their elaboration the aid of an unimpassioned mind—are, except in a very limited sense, incompatible with what is felt to be more important, the vindication of the individual self.

The great part of Makriyannis' post-war life was, then, spent in trying to consolidate the victory which had been won: in trying to reconcile, that is, the irreconcilable, to instil a sense of community into his people. 'Only one thing moves me to write,' he confessed in his memoirs with the same spirit which he demonstrated in his life, 'that this country we all have together, wise and unlearned and rich and poor and politicians and soldiers and the most insignificant men; whoever fought, each one in proportion, we have to live here. Let us then work all together, all of us to preserve it, so neither the powerful say "I" nor the weak. Do you know when each one says "I"? When he fights by himself and makes, or breaks, he says "I"; but when many struggle together and make something, then they say "we".' And in another place he writes in a similar strain:

> The country of each man and his religion are everything and he must give patriotism also and live himself and his brethren with him as honourable men in the community. And then they are called a nation, when they are adorned with patriotic feelings. . . . And because of this, as common country of each man and product of the struggles of the most humble and powerless citizen, everyone has interests in this country, in this religion.

Yet for Makriyannis the problem was even more complicated. He did not simply want anyone to impose the laws and govern the community; the men who made the war must be responsible. For these men had not only been soldiers. They had been inspired by an idea which could be realized only through war, but whose consummation was to be the founding of the new free Greek nation. Yet after the war, these men found themselves pushed to one side to make room for 'foreign' Greeks—Kapodistria, Mavrogordato— men, that is, who had taken no part in the physical struggle for Greece, and whose idea of Greece was strongly coloured by ways of thought borrowed from western Europe. These men became the new political leaders of Greece, often backed by some big power like France or England or Russia. Then when the first king, Otho, arrived, he brought with him his Bavarian court, which established a government of Bavarians, a Bavarocracy. These new rulers, with interfering so-called philhellenes and interfering foreign governments in the background, wished to impose on Greece a 'new order' which took little account of the actual conditions of Greece or of its past. They wished to impose something abstract and *a priori* having no organic relationship to Greek life. This seemed to Makriyannis the final outrage, this spectacle of 'foreigners' devouring the Greece for which he had fought; it inspired some of his finest invective:

> And what has the name of the Greeks done for you, you great men of Europe, you the learned, you the rich? All the learned men of the ancient Greeks, the forefathers of humanity, Lycurgus, Plato, Socrates, Aristides, Themistocles, Leonides, Thrasybulus, Demosthenes and other fathers in general of humanity worked and laboured night and day with virtue, with sincerity, with pure enthusiasm to enlighten mankind. All these great men of the world dwell so many ages in Hades in a dark place and weep and are tormented for the great sufferings which their small unhappy country bears. They being lost, the country Greece was lost also, its name was obliterated. . . . And their pupils the Europeans, in payment for what they owe, give to us the descendants—practice of evil and corruption. Such virtue they have, such enlightenment they give us. A handful of the descendants of these ancient Greeks without rifles and ammunition and the requirements of war tore off the mask of the Grand Seigneur, the Sultan, which he wore on his face and which terrified you the great European. And you paid him tribute, you the mighty, you the rich, you the enlightened, and you called him Grand Seigneur, frightened to call him Sultan. When the poor Greek bare-footed and unclothed fought against him and killed some three hundred thousand of his men, then he (the Sultan) had you the Christians fighting at his side—with your oppositions and your fraud and your deceit and, the first years, with your provisioning of his forts. If you the European had not supplied them, you know where we would have gone with that impetus. After, you filled us with dissension—Dawkins wants us English, Rouan French,

66

Katakazis Russian: and you don't admit a single Greek; each one of you takes his share; and you have us as your puppets; and you say we are unworthy of our freedom, that we do not feel it. The child when it is born is not born with understanding: intelligent people support it and sustain it. . . .

It was in this spirit that Makriyannis took a leading part in the political movement which resulted in the expulsion of the Bavarians. But, alas, though the rulers changed, the old war-leaders did not get any better treatment, and the deceit and the corruption went on. The politicians who took the place of the expelled Bavarians had no more concern for the ideals of the war than those they had succeeded. It is a pathetic sight to watch Makriyannis all those years continuing his implacable search for justice, turning from one party to another always to be disappointed and gaining nothing in the end but the hostility of all parties. It was a process of terrible disillusionment for him. 'Forgive me, readers', he breaks out at one point after describing a typical scene of official callousness:

Forgive me that I have strayed from the subject. Don't think I am bewitched, or that I imagine things, or that I am unjustified. I am sorry to write this; for there were five brothers and only one is spared from the rifle; and their people were so long enslaved and only one woman remains and she hungers; and those from whom she seeks bread want to have their will with her before giving her anything to eat. And this and many other things like this made me stray from the subject; for these things do not liberate the country, they lose it; and I also intend to live in this country; for I have a defenceless family and I am not skilled in flattering the powerful. And I am wretched and weep for my unfortunate country, that for her we spilt our blood vainly.

He retreated more and more into himself, spending many hours digging in the garden of his house at Athens, turning in his distress more and more to God, 'the only true and just governor', as he called him. He had two caves at the bottom of his garden, one of which he made into a kind of a monk's cell, and the other into a shrine with icons, where he prayed much.

It was during these years also that Makriyannis had made those paintings of scenes of the War of Independence which are now recognized to be striking examples of what is called 'primitive' art. Like Makriyannis' memoirs themselves, they were for many years lost and were only brought to light by chance. Makriyannis wanted the battle scenes painted:

I found a French painter and I had him make me in pictures those battles. I didn't know his language. He made two or three. They weren't good. I paid him and he left. After I had dismissed that painter, I sent and they brought from Sparta one who had been in the Revolution, Panagioti Zographos they called him; I brought him and we talked and we agreed on the price of each picture; and he sent and brought his two children; I had them in my house where they worked.'

Makriyannis showed the painter what he wanted, and the painter followed his directions. There were 26 paintings all told. Makriyannis called them 'Thoughts of Makriyannis.'

Makriyannis goes on to describe how he himself made a picture. It was a picture which showed as it were in miniature the whole quality of his love and of his suffering, which showed what one might call his passion:

When the painter had finished the pictures, then I covered one part of my garden with white and black sea-pebbles. I depicted first a circle and around it were lances. That circle was the country, which had been encircled by the lances of tyranny so many centuries. Beneath a dog was depicted; it was the faithful Greek, who had guarded the freedom of his country so many centuries hungry and unclothed in the snow, like the good dog which guards sheep from the wolf. Beneath were two young rams and they fought; thus the Greeks learnt to fight to deliver their country. Beneath is a deer and she suckles her young one. When we have concord, thus our country suckles us. Beneath is a mighty lion and a young wolf devours it; with the strength of God, thus we devoured the Turk. Beneath is a tree loaded with fruit and with a small sack is an unfortunate Greek who fights to gather the fruit of his struggles and evil usurpers prevent him. . . . Beneath is another brave Greek, well-armed; he keeps watch over the freedom of his country, which he liberated with his blood, so that no one dares to harm it. Beneath is a strong lion and he has dug his claws into a luckless Greek and he will tear him open. The Greek calls on God and with his lance he kills the lion. Beneath are the columns of Olympian Zeus and the Gate of Hadrian and the symbol of the owl. Beneath, a dance is taking place; someone with western dress dances with a Greek. . . . The western-dressed person wants his own dance, the Greek wants his own, and soon they will come to blows, because the one cannot learn the dance of the other. Beneath is the war of Greeks and Turks and you see foot-soldiers and cavalry and a host of dead. Beneath are the Greeks of the Revolution, who fought for the freedom of their country, wounded; and there are oxen depicted, carts which bear stones, dung; and the Greeks of the Revolution build the houses and estates of their new over-lords.

Yet all the time as well his uncompromising honesty and his fearlessness in the defence of any victim of injustice made him a figure of dread to all politicians. They imagined his house to be always a centre of sedition and conspiracy; they closed him up in it; they confined him to one of its rooms: 'And now I write with tears,' he says in a despairing, distraught appeal to God which was found among his papers,

and you do not hear us and you do not see us. . . . Imprisoned six months all of us with guards, and I to look at them. And to cry out night and day from my wounds, and to see my afflicted wife and children choked with tears and barefoot. Six months imprisoned in two tiny rooms . . . without doctor, and no one allowed to approach us. . . . My wife sickened and they took her down. . . . I write my defence, no paper speaks for us. . . . After all, they all want us to perish; they make examinations, searches of the house, cellars, roofs, chests, your own icons . . .

In the end they suspected him of a plot to kill the king, and they transferred him to prison. In prison he wrote another defence, but again no paper would publish it:

That I should kill a king—even now when I write it and note it I weep and tremble. . . . When have you heard that I am a beast in society? . . . When have you heard this and other men who have a conscience and call me insane? I am insane, I don't deny it, to the sane, and I will tell you why . . . I have two wounds in the head, another in the throat, another in the arm . . . another in the leg and another in the stomach, and I am bound up in iron and I keep my intestines encased in this. . . . These wounds I received for the country, and when the weather changes, the bitter pain makes me mad . . .

He was tried the following year. There was one witness. The trial lasted five minutes. Makriyannis was condemned to death. From the law-courts, Makriyannis was led to the prison of the military hospital. As he went by the Acropolis he sang. Perhaps it was the song which he had also sung when, during the siege, he had been defending the same Acropolis so that the country whose politicians now condemned him might come into existence:

> The sun had gone down, and the moon was lost
> And the simple Day-Star beside the Pleiades,
> The four they talked together, they in secret talked.
> The sun turned and said to them, the sun turned and spoke:
> 'Yester-eve as I went down behind a little rock,
> I heard the cries of women and men making lament
> For those heroic bodies which lie out in the plain
> And in the pools of blood are all completely sunk.
> For the country they have gone, those luckless ones, to Hades.

But Makriyannis' own torment was not to end so soon. The death sentence was changed to one of life imprisonment; then to imprisonment for 20 years, then for 10 years. Finally, he was let out after three years. But his stay in prison had ruined what strength he had left. And his persecution did not stop:

> After I was freed and I had gone back to my ruined house and to my unfortunate family . . . my wounds broke out afresh. . . . And one Easter . . . I went into the cave which is in my garden to rest. . . . And they threw stones at me and human dung. 'Eat of this General Makriyannis, to satisfy your craving for a regiment.' And from the knocks and because I fell many times to the ground many new wounds opened, and matter flows from them till this day, and blood from before and behind; and I became rotten and full of worms. . . . All this I told to the

70

Council, but they didn't give me a hearing; and this continued till the eve of the feast of the Saviour. . . . And on the same day they beat me much, I was finished, I didn't know whether I was alive or dead . . . I stayed there till nightfall, and on my hands and knees I went and fell on the bed, so that my unfortunate family should not see me . . .

It was the end. He had one more brief period of recognition after the dethronement of the King in 1862, and then, in 1864, he died.

So closed the life of this untutored son of a shepherd who rose to be a General in one of the most crucial wars in his country's history; who, in order to leave a memorial to the heroic spirit and sacrifice of his countrymen, as well as to the betrayal of that spirit and of that sacrifice, learnt to write and wrote what is now recognized to be perhaps the most important prose work of modern Greek literature; and who, finally, because he could not 'bear to see injustice choke justice', because he did not conform where he did not approve, because he was not content merely to affirm what he believed but also demonstrated it in his own life, called down on himself that violence which such people always seem to provoke in those whose power is based, as power so often is, upon corruption and deceit. Men like Makriyannis impress us not through any single aspect of themselves, not through their intellectual ability, or cultural level, or technical skill, or the weight of their learning; they impress us through their total presence, through the ideal of completeness which they embody. Heroic fighter, instinctive sage, writer, seer, and finally martyr—Makriyannis was all of these. It does not matter if he was all of these with the simplicity and lack of sophistication of a man of the people. As Don Quixote, who also had the courage to proclaim and to demonstrate his ideal in defiance of all material reality, has become for Spain a symbol of something that is most noble in her nature, so Makriyannis is already becoming such a symbol for Greece. And such symbols do not remain national. They become universal, for they have the power to stimulate and to enrich the heart and mind of man.

Anghelos Sikelianos and his Vision of Greece

ANGHELOS SIKELIANOS (1884–1951) aspired to be a religious and even a metaphysical poet in the full sense of the word. Consequently his sense of Greece and of being Greek, as well as his understanding of what constitutes the most profound form of Greek tradition, cannot be separated from his appraisal of the spiritual state of the western world of his time. He saw this world as increasingly alienated from those principles which give life significance and beauty and as approaching the condition of a machine out of control and hastening towards destruction. Between man and the creative sources of his life barriers of ideas, creeds, codes, dogmas and programmes had arisen, cutting him off from the deepest roots of his being, destroying his integrity and setting him at war with himself and others.[1] Secular politics had taken the place of sacred institutions, corroding man with bitterness and anger, preventing him from seeing beyond the limits of his material happiness and destroying in him all deeper understanding of life and of the forces which govern it.[2] He no longer occupied that central position on earth which was his birthright. He no longer regarded himself as the microcosm containing in himself all the potentialities of life and upon whose creative activity these potentialities depend for their realization. Instead he had become an instrument, a means, the object of analysis and experiment isolated from that organic framework of relationships with the divine and with the earth to which he rightly belongs. Under such conditions it was inevitable that he should be tossed to and fro on the sea of opposites and contradictions, sometimes trying to resolve them through the invention of abstract philosophical concepts, sometimes treating them as dead mechanical problems and sometimes, unable any longer to endure the stifling and artificial atmosphere he had created around himself with such effort, breaking out into orgies of uncontrollable violence.[3]

Greece—and Sikelianos is speaking here of the Greece of his youth, during the opening years of the twentieth century—had largely been spared this crippling process of rationalization and mechanization. The people of Greece, continuing to live close to the elemental forces of the world, had preserved in however subconscious and rudimentary fashion a vision of the organic wholeness of life. They still retained some of those perceptions and understandings which give life its richness and dignity and which the scientific mentality cannot grasp but can so ruthlessly destroy. The lives of the Greek people during the long years of the Turkish occupation may have been poor, constricted and harsh, but they possessed a poetry and a sense of the mystery and wonder of creation which was rapidly being lost in the West. Moreover, they had enshrined this sense of mystery and wonder and the qualities of thought and feeling which accompanied them in a wealth of song, legend and dance whose origins lay far back in the past. The festivals and ceremonies of the Greek people might be dismissed by the modern mentality as little more than evidence of superstition and primitiveness; but for those who participated in them they were the means of contact with the forces of life and death, and were capable of raising the imagination of men above the sphere of mere economic self-interest and other biological and material considerations.

Now, however, this process of rationalization and mechanization was beginning to infect Greece and Greek life. The political leaders of Greece, blind to the real values and roots of their country's history and seduced by the technical mastery of the West, were doing what they could to bring Greece into line with western development. The speed at which this change was taking place had increased during the years of the 1914–18 war and its aftermath. Those years, crucial for the whole world, were even more crucial for

Greece. They had witnessed a disastrous break in the traditional ways of life. Thought, action and feeling had been torn out of their true and natural context—their context of nature and the people. It was this people, linked organically to the earth, that had preserved through the centuries the myth and meaning of life against the attempts of the parasitic growth, 'civilization', to destroy it.

One of the weapons used in its attacks by so-called civilization was its secular and profane system of education. The adoption by Greece of western methods of education was having the same effects in Greece as it had already had in the West. The organic sense of life was being shattered into countless unconnected fragments. The traditions of the Greek people were being disrupted and a scientific attitude to nature was taking their place. A system of learning which made extreme demands on the purely mechanical and sterile processes of memory had the effect of absorbing all the spontaneous movements of body and soul of the younger generations. Moreover, those who went abroad to study and who then returned to Greece and to that way of life from which they had issued, now looked down on it from the height of their sophistication as if from some unbridgeable distance, or at best regarded it as something decorative at the margin of their imagined civilization; and, anaemic as they were, they sought to absorb from it, and from the blood and spirit of the people, that nourishment which their own vacuous lives so conspicuously lacked.[4]

Yet already 'the inexhaustible clamour of the machines and inventions and theories of the West' was showing signs of exhaustion, and 'the walls which its arrogant civilization had created round the soul of man'[5] were beginning to crack. Again, the 1914-18 war had marked a crucial stage in this process. Man was beginning to awaken once more, to become conscious of his powers and of his destiny. The veil of this artificial civilization which had covered everyone's eyes had been rent, and at the heart of creation man was suddenly able to perceive himself anew. A change in man's sensibility, in his ways of thought, was beginning to take place. He was becoming aware once more of universal issues; he was beginning to free himself from a one-sided appreciation of life; and those dead circles of thought, which had prevented his access to any real understanding of things, were disappearing from his spiritual horizon. In other words, all those conceptions, false values, theories, systems and anomalies which together made up the civilization of the West, were in retreat like a corrupt language before a new awareness and restitution of life.[6] This of course was a direct consequence of the decay of that civilization itself. For when life, and especially the life of modern industrial cities, had reached the point of degeneration which it now had, and when the spirit of destruction reigned everywhere, nothing was more necessary than that a few, who understood the significance of the signs around them, should seek once more to recover contact with the uncorrupted sources of life, with those principles on which human existence depends and which had been so fatally lost.[7]

What Sikelianos understood by sources and principles of life had been indicated by Goethe when he spoke of 'The Mothers', those strange powers who dwell in the depths of the universe, in the ever-empty farness of man's nature; and by Blake when he spoke of the Giants who formed this world into its sensual existence and now seem to live in it in chains. It was severance from these inner sources which are the ground not only of his own existence but of the existence of all that is, that had resulted in the dislocated state in which man now found himself. The only way then through which man could recover his integrity and could re-establish his equilibrium and his sense of beauty and purpose was by reversing the process. Beyond the ruins of the contemporary scientific and industrial world he had to regain contact with those powers who dwell in the depths:

We must address ourselves to the sources. We must address ourselves first of all to our own soul. We must measure its thirst, its pain, its patience. And when we are assured, when we feel that this thirst burns our heart like a desert, when the pain and the patience are welded secretly within us into a single feeling,

75

which is at once contrition and sweetness and courage—then we must address ourselves to the creators. We must search for the spring of human sensibility and try to enter—not now out of profane curiosity but out of concern for our deliverance—that holy circle where those great, living, authentic creators of all ages, to whatever level they belong, have, we feel, some common bond between them. We must try to approach them not through what in an external sense we are in the habit of calling their work, whether this is religion, or poetry, or art, or thought or even science, and which is set out statically in churches or museums or books for us to respect and admire; but we must try to approach them in their very depths, in their original and existential depths, where the wound of their universal and historical and individual being is always open: that secret, open wound, that generative wound which, as the womb of a mother that night and day nourishes the embryo with her own blood, itself nourishes the work that they were born to bring for all of us into the light and into life.[8]

Through a concrete and conscious animation of his own interior energies man would again re-establish contact with the original sources of life, and would achieve the regeneration for which he sought. It would be a regeneration in. which the inner and outer aspect of things would be seen as the manifestation of a single generative power—a power that is at the same time the most primitive and simple aspect of man's interior world. It would be a regeneration that raised afresh all aspects of life to a level from which they had fallen or been scattered, and that welded all traditions into one archetypal tradition of man, all myths into one Myth.[9]

Sikelianos felt that the understanding of life which he opposed to the dominant tendencies of the modern world had some affinity with that of ancient Greece. He felt that in a certain period in the history of ancient Greece this understanding had been recognized and to a partial extent realized. It lay in fact at the basis of the creative effort of that period. It was then that life had been consciously, if incompletely, related to a tradition that embodied those principles which Sikelianos had come to regard as the most profound and most sacred principles of existence, those which modern civilization had so effectively smothered. Sikelianos regarded such a recognition of a historical counterpart or such an alignment with a spiritual tradition as a prerequisite for the full development of the individual creative spirit. Without it, this spirit was in danger of self-destruction. It was likely to founder in subjective chaos or in precisely that state of constriction from which its development would signify release: 'For as the eagle,' he wrote,[10]

> each time it wishes to raise itself from the earth must first walk a certain specific distance (because if it does not have this requisite distance free before it, it will remain a prisoner of its own wings), so the human spirit . . . if it fails to feel beneath it a certain perspective of spiritual history to which it corresponds, is similarly in danger, as it has been so many times over the centuries, of remaining subject to the constriction of the arena from which it aspires continually to save itself.

That 'certain perspective of spiritual history' which Sikelianos regarded as the counterpart to his own understanding, or that tradition in which he saw the principles of this understanding enshrined, was, we have said, connected with the world of ancient Greece. But the standards of that world had, he thought, been misunderstood and misrepresented by the modern western world. They had been confused with 'the low turbid and bastard currents of thought and morality of that profane fabrication which is called "Greco-Latin civilization".'[11] 'Since the death of ancient Greece,' he wrote,[12]

> a heavy and almost unliftable curtain has fallen between the ancient and the modern world and has covered the intellectual, aesthetic and psychic radiance of Hellenism: aesthetic rationalism which, under the common name of 'paganism', issued from Rome and her politico-religious pandemonium, was reinforced by the Italian Renaissance and was set up on a pedestal by the eighteenth century. It is this standard which has been established as the absolute criterion of the ancient world for European civilisation.

As far as ancient Greek art was concerned, western understanding had not gone beyond Vitruvius, and as far as its creative impulse was concerned, it had stopped on the threshold of the prosaic and static conceptions of Aristotle.[13] There had been of course exceptions to this general rule of misunderstanding. Keats—and especially the Keats of *Hyperion*—had been one. Goethe had been another; but Goethe, like Winckelmann before him, had seen Greece behind Rome and so had been prevented from any deep appreciation of her genius. The two western Europeans who had perhaps come closest to this appreciation had been Hölderlin and Nietzsche. They had lived the miracle of ancient Greece as it were by telepathy; but even so their penetration into the mystery had been incomplete. They had lacked the one thing that might have consummated it: actual physical contact with the land of Greece. And, Sikelianos concludes,

it may have been precisely the non-consummation of their spiritual marriage with this land—where the light itself, for those who are not blind or who do not take it for granted, is spirit and continual revelation; where the sea is an eternal melody and the soil, each soil, a holy sculpture—it may have been precisely this non-consummation of the marriage they longed for with this land·that eventually plunged their minds into the infernal darkness.[14]

What was this vision of ancient Greece at its greatest which Sikelianos regarded as habitually misunderstood by the West? He described it and how he attained it in an autobiographical note.[15] Almost all his life he had lived among the peasant people of Greece. Among them he had perceived here and there, in the language, in the customs, in the song and dance, reflections of a genuine and autonomous spiritual tradition. But they had been only reflections restricted to the limits of a particular local environment. Then, in addition to the peasant people, there were the ancient monuments. The landscape around him was full of ruins and these ruins spoke a language distinct from all others in the world. He knew the language of the people well; but how was he to learn this other language, the language of the ruins? His admiration alone would not teach him it. He had to have recourse to books. But to what books? The ramifications of Greek thought throughout the centuries were enormous. But where was its trunk? That was the great question. Was there a single individual, poet or philosopher, whose work had enshrined the essence of ancient Greece—that Greece which stood above all Asiatic vague immensities and above the religious, political, institutional, philosophical and artistic misrepresentations of later times? He was counselled to study Plato above all. Plato, he was told, was a bridge between the old world and the new. To him had descended the full Orphic and Pythagorean tradition; he had inspired the Alexandrian neo-Platonists and had strengthened the thought of the Greek Fathers; it was his work that had blown a breath of creative vitality into the West at the time of the Renaissance and had been the basis of the idealism of Winckelmann and Goethe. It could be a living force for the present time.

Indeed, Plato did appear to have expressed much of the essence of ancient Greece. But, as he studied him, Sikelianos began to perceive that the Greece his work embodied was not Greece at the height of her creative powers, when the rhythms and principles of her spiritual tradition had been fully realized and liberated; rather it was Greece at the moment of decline, beautiful and rich but nevertheless in decline. He sensed, too, beneath the beauty of the language the agony and nostalgia with which Plato himself had sought to recapture the Greece of the true rhythms and principles and how he had been too late to grasp them in their essence, too late to come before the Greek people with the strength of a true spiritual teacher. His action was but on the level of theory. Protected nearly always behind the shield of Socrates, he was able to give his teaching a dramatic form which no doubt appealed in a general way to the Athenians but did not affect them vitally. The conclusions of his earlier and more experimental dialogues were invariably negative. His strength was exhausted not so much in illuminating those principles whose validity he was coming increasingly to

79

recognize, but in clearing the logical ground by means of his dialectic, so that, as he thought, they might reveal themselves of their own accord to his readers. His already 'over-aestheticized' contemporary Athenian surroundings had stifled within him that direct spiritual strength possessed by his spiritual ancestors, the pre-Socratics, in whom understanding, feeling and power had constituted a unity to which thought and action were subordinate.

Yet Plato's inner struggle was concerned precisely with the question of how to realize this unity for himself and how to incarnate it in his surroundings. The attempt on the part of the pre-Socratics and above all of the Pythagoreans to create a pan-Hellenic and universal spiritual unity always haunted him. He aspired to make a similar attempt in his turn. But it was when he came to make it that he revealed how far short he fell of a true realization of the principles of the tradition. It was because of this that instead of coming forth before the Greek people as a true spiritual teacher, he addressed himself instead to a foreign tyrant, in the hope that he would impose his ideas on Greece. As for these ideas themselves—at least as they are expressed in the *Republic*—they represented an idealized and despotic form of communism, an excessive attachment to Sparta which revealed all the thirst and nostalgia of his epoch for a discipline that could not be achieved in his contemporary social environment. His proposals for the creation of the ideal citizen were often sound, but they were not co-ordinated organically and lacked an over-riding and living unity.

However, without Plato we would have lost not only the immortal artist, not only the dramatic portrait of Socrates and the unique expression of the intellectual and moral climate of an age, but also a considerable part of those elements which without doubt constituted the most profound tradition of the ancient Greek world—elements which Plato himself expounded above all in his later dialogues. It was Plato's limitation that he was unable to assimilate and to simplify these elements to the point at which he could reveal them not only through the prism of theory but also as principles of a communal teaching capable of living application. It was for this reason that his great influence, as it was shaped by the neo-Platonists of Alexandria at a most critical time for Hellenism, when the ancient world was advancing towards the new world, remained largely on the level of theory. It was not able to counteract the Judaic element in Christianity and so to confer on Christianity a cultural dimension with which Hellenism alone was capable of endowing it.

These observations about Plato's relationship to the spiritual tradition of ancient Greece apply to an even greater degree in the case of Aristotle. Aristotle's contact with the creative principles of that tradition was slight and uncertain. His work was encyclopaedic, above all analytical and descriptive. He was concerned not so much to synthesize as to classify and distinguish, without showing the governing and essential link between things. This is not because his enormous critical powers were incapable of discerning that link, but because it had only an abstract significance for him. Consequently, his metaphysics, his poetics, his grammar and his politics remain subordinate to a method in which strictly logical categories are allowed to determine the nature of ontological realities and in which 'being', 'becoming' and 'doing' appear to be in essence separated.

These remarks that apply in varying degrees to Plato and Aristotle did not apply to the same extent to the pre-Socratics; and it was in the Greece of the pre-Socratics that Sikelianos saw that tradition, with whose principles he felt his own vision had some affinity, most fully realized. The writings of the pre-Socratics, he felt, were free from those dichotomies which were already beginning to fragment Plato's thought. The metaphysician did not stifle the poet or the poet the human being. Nature, phenomenon and noumenon were linked together inseparably, being seen in their relationship to a deeper and more universal principle. This principle was identified for Sikelianos with that feminine or maternal principle whose presence at the heart of the whole Aegean civilization had been one of the more important subjects of recent historical research. As he himself wrote:[16]

> Thanks to this, we unexpectedly remember once more the full extension of the maternal principle whose supreme value has been either forgotten or tragically distorted by the false and artificial masculinity of later civilizations based not on our own soul and our own power but on arms, money and cold life-destroying machines. For this eternal principle is not merely the symbol of that hidden cause of superficial so-called 'physical phenomena' which we define by the exceptionally inadequate term 'reproduction'; it also contains within itself treasures of protection, tenderness, inner development and love, treasures without which man would long ago have disappeared from the face of the earth—a fate which it were far better he should have suffered if he cannot find those treasures in a positive and substantial manner once more.

Although a recognition of this feminine principle was crucial to a proper understanding of the pre-Socratic tradition, the scope of that tradition was the complete liberation of man from the bondage of fear and death through an integration of the limited individual ego with the deeper Self which is the centre both of man's life and of all that is, and may be described as the masculine pole of existence. In other words, the understanding of life enshrined in the pre-Socratic tradition was one that affirmed and reconciled the masculine and feminine principles of life, and that preserved a sense both of life's organic wholeness and of the need for individual initiation into a more than individual state of existence. Sikelianos regarded Orphism and the cult of Dionysos, the teaching of Pythagoras, the mysteries of Eleusis and the mantic centre at Delphi as four of the main expressions of this tradition. In them he saw embodied what was essentially the same understanding of life, an understanding which transcended the limits of their particular age, affirmed that all men are brothers and proclaimed a unity which embraced not only all mankind but all living creatures, from the grain of sand to the most spiritual form of being. In this view of things, man occupies a central position in that he is, as it were, the channel of communication between higher and lower states of existence, between the invisible and the visible, heaven and earth; and all levels and states of being have their meeting-place in him. The shifting, changing scenes of the visible world are the varying expression of a deeper reality. The world is not the plaything of a blind and indiscriminate chance; it is the expression of a harmonious purpose, although this purpose is often obscured or disrupted by a defect in man's own inner organization. The supreme reality dwells in all things and moves them all. It is formless, impersonal, pure and passionless and yet at the same time the warm full-blooded life in the heart of man.

Sikelianos did not claim that this tradition of which Orphism, the teachings of Pythagoras and the Eleusinian mysteries were an expression was of native Greek origin. He looked eastwards, to Asia, for the source of the deep religious currents of life that had flowed westward and penetrated into Europe—'the venerable Asia', as he calls her,[17] 'that beneath the obscure marks of her numberless civilizations seems to have preserved not only her own secret but the secret of a brotherly relationship between us within a more ancient civilization that has vanished.' He was well aware of the 'Oriental background against which classical culture arose and from which it was never completely isolated save in the minds of classical scholars.'[18] In particular he looked to India and to the great religious teachings of the *Vedas* and the *Upanishads*; and he felt that the legend of Demeter's wanderings and of her final settlement at Eleusis concealed a historical process in which, after a long period of persecution and expulsion from one country to another, representatives of this old spiritual wisdom of mankind had at last found a resting-place on Greek soil.

Sikelianos was a poet and not a scholar; and in any case it is impossible to chart the diffusion of religious ideas with any accuracy. But much of what Sikelianos believed in this connection is supported by what little evidence has survived. For instance, Orpheus was said to have been a Thracian, a prophet of a religious school or sect with a way of life, a

83

mystical theology and a system of purificatory and expiatory rites.[19] Thracian seers are reported by Herodotos to be interested in natural philosophy and speculative theology.[20] They had much in common with the Brahmins. Indeed, 'it is difficult to dissociate . . . the philosophy of ancient Thrace from the Brahmins of India.'[21] Similarly, the myth of Demeter and Persephone and the *nekuia* of Homer had an Asiatic origin.[22] Aurobindo Ghosh connects the *Vedas* with Orphic and Eleusinian worship. The Veda was a mystery religion:

> The hypothesis I propose is that the *Rg-Veda* is itself the one considerable document that remains to us from the early period of human thought of which the historical Eleusinian and Orphic mysteries were the failing remnants, when the spiritual and psychological knowledge of the race was concealed, for reasons now difficult to determine, in a veil of concrete and material figures and symbols which protected the sense from the profane and revealed it to the initiated.[23]

A similar hypothesis could be proposed in relation to Pythagoras. It was said of Pythagoras and his followers that 'every distinction they lay down as to what should be done or not done aims at communion with the divine. This is their starting point; their whole life is ordered with a view to following God and it is the governing principle of their philosophy.'[24] Iamblichus, the biographer of Pythagoras, writes that Pythagoras travelled widely and studied the teachings of Egyptians, Assyrians and Brahmins. 'It is not too much to assume that the curious Greek, who was a contemporary of Buddha, and it may be of Zoroaster too, would have acquired more or less exact knowledge of the East in that age of intellectual fermentation, through the medium of Persia.'[25] In any case, 'almost all the theories, religious, philosophical and mathematical taught by the Pythagoreans were known in India in the sixth century B.C., and the Pythagoreans, like the Jains and the Buddhists, refrained from the destruction of life and eating meat and regarded certain vegetables such as beans as taboo.'[26] In short, 'whether or not we accept the hypothesis of direct influence from India through Persia on the Greeks, a student of Orphic and Pythagorean thought cannot fail to see that the similarities between it and the Indian religion are so close as to warrant our regarding them as expressions of the same view of life. We can use the one system to interpret the other.'[27]

Of particular importance for Sikelianos where this spiritual teaching of ancient Greece is concerned was the rôle of poetry and the place of the poet in the religious life of his people. It was a rôle and a place which he himself aspired to create in modern Greece. To understand them, Sikelianos maintained, we have to enlarge our normal attitude to poetry. We have become used to seeing in poetry

an aspect of life's expression which consoles us for other harsh aspects, an interruption of the heavy sense of time, a 'nepenthic' drink which offers us an unexpected alchemy and which, when we taste it, frees us for a little from the constriction of the everyday world, whether of life or thought—from everything which, beginning with calculation, ends with the inescapable bankruptcy that awaits whatever is calculated. We inhale it like a momentary breath of enormous freedom, as a fish which, leaping suddenly from the water, tastes for a second the air outside only to fall back again at once into its huge prison.[28]

Such an attitude towards poetry is good as far as it goes. But it does not go very far. The poet, in the fullest sense of the word, has a more important function than is implied in this attitude to his work:

The poet, if he is truly a poet, is well aware that through poetry he struggles to attain genuine liberation. He does not try to attain this for himself only, but as an initial stage in the liberation of all mankind.[29]

The poet and his poetry stand as an essential link between human society and the universal principles of life, revealing them to mankind. Poetry is

the only absolutely synthetic Idea which, transcending religions, philosophies and politics, advances like a star through history, shedding its light on ever-wider horizons of reality. Its mission begins where dogma ends, where philosophies founder and where politics reveal their incapacity to grasp the deeper levels of human and historical life. In other words poetry begins on the other side of those barriers set up and still being set up by creeds, philosophies and politics to help in the tragic preservation of the base values of what is still a lop-sided conventional civilization.[30]

The source of poetry is, or should be, divine inspiration. The poet is also the prophet. He is the seer who is also the mystagogue to his people.

Sikelianos is here invoking an understanding of the poet's status and function which was once fully recognized and which has never entirely been lost. Among the Brahmins, among the mantic classes of ancient Gaul, with the seers and poets of ancient Ireland, in early Thrace, in ancient Greece and doubtless in Etruria, this understanding prevailed:

> Everywhere the gift of poetry is inseparable from divine inspiration. Everywhere this inspiration carries with it knowledge—whether of the past, in the form of history and genealogy; of the hidden present, in the form commonly of scientific information; or of the future, in the form of poetic utterance in the narrower sense. Always this knowledge is accompanied by music, whether of song or instrument. Music is everywhere the medium of communication with spirit. Invariably we find that the poet and seer attributes his inspiration to contact with supernatural powers, and his mood during prophetic utterance is exalted and remote from that of his normal existence. Generally we find that a recognized process is in vogue by which the prophetic mood can be induced at will. The lofty claims of the poet and seer are universally admitted, and he himself holds a high status wherever he is found.[31]

It appears that such an understanding of the poet and of the poet's function arises spontaneously when the communication between man and the divine is still of paramount importance and when inspiration is still a living reality. As a society loses this creative spiritual orientation and becomes secularized, so this understanding diminishes until in periods of almost complete 'materialism' it all but disappears.

In that period of Greek history which Sikelianos in some

measure regarded as 'archetypal', society still possessed a spiritual orientation sufficiently coherent to produce poets of a character and calibre equal to the high calling of the inspired prophet and seer. 'In this period,' Sikelianos wrote,[32]

> the poet is not the organ of a particular set of ideas or facts but he is a person who fulfils a unique and fundamental educational mission which embraces all facts and ideas. Poetry, that is to say, is not only an art; it is the complete art, the art of arts. It is a force which at the impulsion of the divine Logos not only combines all musical "modes", like the Lydian, the Phrygian, the Dorian and the Aeolian, but also inspires the Amphictyonic Councils and the constitution of the most creative and civilizing institutions.

Two poets above all in ancient Greece appeared to Sikelianos to have fulfilled this role of educator and mystagogue. The first was Pindar. Particularly significant was Pindar's association with Delphi. Delphi was one of the spiritual founts of ancient Greece, a centre of traditional wisdom and inspiration. The function of Delphi was to disseminate this wisdom and inspiration among the peoples and cities of Greece, so that life should be in harmony with the underlying principles of the universe. The poetry of Pindar—the Delphic poet—represented one continuous effort toward this end. The lofty spirit of this poetry rose like a spring wind summoning the whole of Greece to a creative flowering with a language and a humanity which no other poet has achieved. It possesses this quality because Pindar draws it either from his own subjective experience or from his deep sympathy with the individual or individuals that he presents. For, sensitive to the fullest degree, Pindar never separates in his work conflict from compassion, form from content, soul from body. In other words, Pindar's counsel is never dry, ethical advice but a means whereby he can help those to whom he gives it towards an even deeper joy and fulfilment.[33]

The other ancient Greek poet whom Sikelianos regarded as being in the line of the great tradition of prophets and seers was Aeschylus. He saw Aeschylus standing in the same relation to Eleusis and to the Eleusinian Mysteries as Pindar to Delphi and to the Delphic teaching. Like Delphi, Eleusis had proclaimed 'the great mystagogic, organic and universal symbols of the inner creative unity of man with man, of the individual with the universe and more directly with the earth, of peoples and races with all the peoples and races of the world.'[34] Aeschylus' great endeavour, like that of Pindar, had been to manifest these same symbols to the peoples and cities of Greece, especially, where Aeschylus was concerned, to Athens and to the Athenians. The great plays of Aeschylus had been attempts, on a scale wider than at the sanctuary of Eleusis, to initiate the people of Athens into the highest mysteries of life, each individual according to the level of his particular understanding. This integration could not be achieved only by heroic resistance and prophetic power; it also required complete initiation into the mysteries of this and the other world, until finally the purified soul was able to experience that contact with the eternal Logos which the Eleusinian hierophants called Epiphany or Attainment of Vision and which gives man the strength to overcome fate and to play a creative part in the development of the life of those around him.[35]

It was through the use of myth that these two great poets of ancient Greece, Pindar and Aeschylus, had sought to liberate man from the shackles of time and place and of his own limitations and to make him conscious of his true nature. Myth, as Sikelianos saw it, and as he understood these earlier poets to see it, is not simply a means whereby the poet is able to indulge a certain playfulness of fancy; nor is it a rhetorical or metaphorical device. It is on the contrary the spontaneous creation of the human soul which is working in a certain direction and towards a definite end: the revelation of the spiritual life. Sikelianos quoted with approval the words of Schelling:

> Mythology contains within it all religious truth. Religion is not mythology, as modern scholars imagine. On the contrary, mythology is religion. All myths are true. They are not fab-

rications about what does not exist, but revelations of what always exists. Persephone of the mysteries of Eleusis does not merely symbolize, but is truly for those who can understand her a living being. The same can be said where all the gods are concerned.[36]

The true poet, when he creates a myth, not only makes a pattern, he also proclaims a truth; and he not only proclaims a truth, he also provides the means through which the truth he proclaims can be realized. It was this that Pindar had learnt from Delphi: that the myth is not something ornamental or arbitrary but the means whereby the human soul can attain, step by step, an understanding of the mysteries and of its own powers. On the poetic level, the soul creates with images, but these images are disposed according to a predetermined pattern. The true poet is consequently opposed to disturbing this pattern, because it represents those steps by which man is able to advance beyond a purely mythological awareness of things and to penetrate into that realm from which the myths themselves are born. The uninitiated poet, on the other hand, who has but a confused idea of the significance of myth, will disarrange the pattern in the belief that thereby he is expressing more directly his own individual feelings and so is liberated from them—something which is not in fact the case since, in making those images serve merely his own ego, he remains captive to that ego. He ignores that truth in the light of which Pindar had set out on his great creative mission: the truth that behind the gods and all myths is concealed the inexhaustible source of myths and gods; and it is from this source that the true poet, according to his degree of illumination and receptivity, must derive the models for his poetry.[37]

This ancient and noble understanding of the poet as the inspired teacher and mystagogue with his profound sense of the nature and function of myth was lost in ancient Greece as society itself lost touch with the principles of the great tradition. Dissociated from these principles, the human mind began to evolve its own dualistic criteria, opening a chasm

89

between the life of poetry and the poetry of life, between the image and the act, between the Logos and history. The centre could not hold and the worlds fell apart. This was the tragedy, the 'crucifixion', as Sikelianos saw it, that Aeschylus suffered. His great effort to initiate his people into the mysteries met with less and less response. The weight and scope of his vision were beyond the grasp of the now degenerating Athenian world. The Athenians became hostile to him, and they ceased to follow him as they had followed him at first. His solemn hieratic tetralogy was too much for them. They preferred the artistic Sophocles, who was less aware than Aeschylus of the 'limitless spiritual frontier of the world', and did not know that ancient mystagogic tradition of the sacred history of humanity. Sophocles' plays, with their great beauty, flattered and satisfied the people. Their scope became local, with unity of time and place, with a symmetry that was easy to understand and to enjoy. Of what use now was that terrible, often Sibylline and obscure standard of Aeschylus?[38]

It appeared to Sikelianos that something happened in the realm of the human spirit somewhere round the turn of the sixth century B.C. which affected the whole future development of western society. The great tradition of the ancient world was broken and a new and less exalted age began. Greece had found the highest point of her genius in the poet but now she was no longer capable of realizing this genius. Shortly after the death of Pindar the drama of political disruption began. In giving her the rhythms of an eternal teaching, spiritual, political and aesthetic, the poet had given Greece everything. But now she was no longer worthy to maintain the poet's testament in its integrity. Poet, priest and prophet were no longer united in a single person, and poetry could no longer stamp life with the luminous seal of its universal and communal mission. More than the divorce of any other values, this divorce of poetry and life gradually produced that rootless and purposeless dispersion of human energies from which we still suffer. The great achievement of the whole history of ancient Greece, which was precisely this perfect marriage of poetry and life, now fell away to nothing. For this reason, and in spite of all the honour given it, the testament of the two greatest poets of Greece, Pindar and Aeschylus, has gone largely unrecognized in what concerns its central mission: the preservation of this marriage of poetry and life above every other manifestation of human energy. It is from this point of view that the great question remains: will poetry and life ever come together again in this world, and will the world ever again transcend its vain and ephemeral pursuits through an awareness of a spiritual teaching which it has always been the function of true poetry and of the true poet to communicate?[39]

The question was not rhetorical. Sikelianos, we have said, aspired to be a metaphysical poet in the full sense of the word, and to assume the rôle fulfilled in ancient Greece by such poets as Pindar and Aeschylus. He saw those poets as the representatives of a tradition of spiritual knowledge in which the highest values of the Greek world had been enshrined and which therefore constituted the Greek tradition *par excellence*, embracing and in a certain way transcending all later spiritual traditions, such as that of Christianity, which had taken root in this world. Of this tradition, the traditions of the peasant people of modern Greece were, Sikelianos thought, a rapidly disappearing reflection. These people were the direct heirs of the ancient tradition, the oral library, so to speak, of Greece's most profound culture. Their beliefs were a relic of former knowledge. Their collective memory was a repository of images and symbols whose true significance could be rediscovered only through a conscious integration to and alignment with the metaphysical tradition which they once expressed. It followed that for Sikelianos a precondition of fulfilling his task (of being a *Greek* poet, expressing the highest *Greek* values) was precisely such an integration and alignment. His problem, as he put it,[40] was how to achieve essential contact with and understanding of this metaphysical tradition of the ancient Greek world; how to 'dig up again, out of the earth of time, Greece's most ancient, universal and historical foundations.'[41] Unless he could do this, his creative life would founder in pure subjectivism or in the slavish imitation of western models—a fate similar to that which modern Greece herself would suffer unless she could become conscious of her true spiritual roots. Sikelianos recalled that when as a youth he had been 'so enthusiastic about the freedom of modern Greece, which I then saw only in its epic form and regarded as complete, not suspecting that without a fundamental spiritual autonomy freedom is meaningless', his father had situated both the personal and the national issue in a single perspective:

> Truly, my child, we have escaped from the Turk, thanks to the strength of our great heroes and to the intervention of European powers. . . . To this extent we are not now slaves; but, for reasons you will understand later, we are involuntarily and totally dependents of the West, of its morality, its politics and everything else. This is more dangerous even than slavery for a people so recently liberated. Slavery in general has but one form and so the form of resistance is óne. But dependency, however inescapable (for we have suddenly entered the sphere of a civilization from which we have been cut off for several centuries), grows and will continue to grow until we awake from our lethargy and look around us and within us, at what we are and where we are, and see how parasitic our whole life has become and how incapable of creative reaction. Our true relationships as individuals and as a people with our own environment—physical, intellectual and institutional relation-ships—are today little more than hypothetical. To free herself truly, then, Greece must first rediscover those relationships and above all she must rediscover her whole interior spirit, that spirit which secretly governs her history and which in past ages has fertilized in her whatever is good and great; and she must make this spirit entirely her own, not any longer merely with words, but through its application to every aspect of her life. Then, yes, and only then will Greece be truly free.[42]

This statement gives the measure of what Sikelianos regarded as his task. Through his poetry he sought to resuscitate a whole world of thought and feeling, a whole complex of relationships and experiences which had been buried beneath habits and modes deriving from alien sources; and through his educational activity he sought to apply these resuscitated forms to the alienated and dispossessed Greek society of his own times. To what extent he was successful in this attempt to unite poetry and life is a question which lies beyond the scope of this essay.[43] He himself might have echoed the words of Hölderlin's *Hyperion*: 'Who can abide it, whom does it not lay low, as a hurricane lays low young woods, when the terrifying splendour of Antiquity seizes him as it seized me, when, as for me, the surroundings are lacking in which he might gain a strengthening self-reliance.'[44] In this respect, the crucial lack in Sikelianos' surroundings may be indicated by recalling that if, as he maintained, Pindar and Aeschylus received authority for their creative mission through their dependence on those initiatory centres of Delphi and Eleusis to which they were so intimately related, he himself was attached to no such centre. In his struggle to affirm that the roots of 'Greekness' lay in the pre-Socratic age and to rediscover the true spiritual significance of this age, he bypassed, as it were, the fact that the actual living spiritual tradition of the Greek world had been for close on two thousand years that of Christianity; and consequently he did not adequately perceive that the only real possibility for Greece's spiritual regeneration must depend upon a revival of her tradition in its Christian form. But in the end, Sikelianos' endeavour is not to be judged in the light of his success or failure in bringing it to fruition in practical terms. In the end it is to be judged only in the light of the imaginative coherence and intellectual probity of that vision on which it was based and without which it would not have existed.

George Seferis 1900-1971: The Man and his Poetry

THE DEATH OF A POET is always a kind of resurrection for his poetry. The poetry is now free from its creator; it stands alone, by itself, and as time passes so it becomes more detached from the circumstances and the human being that gave it birth. It becomes one further testimony to man's great struggle to prevent human life and civilization itself from sinking into turpitude, inertia and spiritual death. This is as it should be, and we must not complain that it is what will happen to Seferis' poetry. But before it happens I would like to say something about this particular poet who, as most of us born into this age, suffered his full share of the idiocies of gods and men, but who unlike most of us was also gifted with the voice to express something of what that means.

Who was he, this man, what was he like? A deep, unhurried, meditative man, solid and yet most mobile, fluid almost. I like to think of him sometimes as a kind of sea-creature, a whale or a dolphin, that shows its back above the element it lives in; and certainly he was very much of the sea—was he not born, as he says, 'close to the sea that I wind and unwind on my fingers?'[1] Images of the sea occur and recur throughout his poetry:

> swimming in the waters of this sea
> and of that sea . . .

(21)

he writes, or:

> The sea that embittered us is deep and unexplored
> and unfolds a boundless calm . . .

(31)

Or he echoes the cry of Clytaemnestra:

94

The sea, the sea, who will be able to drain it dry?

(7)

Yes, his poetry is full of the sea, of shells and sea-caves:

> In the sea caves
> there's a thirst, there's a love
> there's an ecstasy
> all hard like shells
> you can hold them in your hand . . .

(193)

It is full of the smell of tar and the taste of brine and salt, of old ports, of old ships, sunk ships, like the *Thrush,* sunk off the island of Poros during the 1939-45 war:

> . . . a small wreck; the masts,
> broken, swayed at odd angles deep underwater, like tentacles,
> or the memory of dreams, marking the hull:
> vague mouth of some huge dead sea-monster
> extinguished in the water . . .

(327)

It is full of the sea and of people of the sea, sailors of his childhood 'who, leaning on their nets with winter coming on and the wind angering, used to recite, with tears in their eyes, the song of *Erotokritos'*; or like his friend, the poet Captain Antoniou—one of those, he writes, who 'carried with him that rather vague feeling which we love in those very few people who help us to live in our land, and which differentiates us, if difference there is, from other nations in the world.' And he adds: 'I should venture to call this feeling the bitter cancer of Hellenism.' And it is full too, his poetry, of the echoes of voyages not yet begun or of voyages that will never finish—*Log-Books* was the title he gave to several collections of his poems, and one of his main *personae* is a certain Stratis Thalassinos—Stratis the Mariner.

Yet this sense of the sea—this sense of journeying across the sea, of searching for one knows not what, for some lost world or for some inexplicable beauty which just eludes us—this sense, Seferis seems to suggest, is not merely his own private experience. It is something we all share. It is an aspect of the human condition. 'What are they after, our souls,' he asks in a fairly early poem, one of the sections from a long sequence published in 1935 to which he gave the title *Mythistorima*:

What are they after, our souls, travelling
on the decks of decayed ships
crowded in with sallow women and crying babies
unable to forget themselves either with the flying fish
or with the stars that the masts point out at their tips—
grated by gramophone records
committed to non-existent pilgrimages unwillingly,
murmuring broken thoughts from foreign languages?

What are they after, our souls, travelling
on rotten brine-soaked timbers
from harbour to harbour?

Shifting broken stones, breathing in
the pine's coolness with greater difficulty each day
swimming in the waters of this sea
and of that sea
without the sense of touch
without men
in a country that is no longer ours
nor yours.

We knew that the islands were beautiful
somewhere round about here where we're groping—
a little nearer or a little farther,
the slightest distance.

(21)

But Seferis was not only of the sea. Perhaps it would be better to describe him as amphibian. For he was very much of the land too—of the earth, earthy: a very rooted man. He liked the physical touch of things, he liked to test out his thought and his feeling against the pulse of rock and tree. He had a great sense of intimacy with things of the physical world. I remember the day that I first met him, a few years after the end of the Second World War. It was on one of those occasions when he was back in Greece for a few months, an interlude before setting out again to take up yet

96

another diplomatic post abroad. It was also during the time when he was discovering the drama of the Greek light—the 'angelic and black' light of Attica, as he called it. We walked on the dry stony paths between the fruit and vegetable gardens lying on the outskirts of Kifisia, towards Mount Parnes. And I remember how I was struck even then by the way this man, whom I'd always thought of as a man of the city, fitted into this Greek landscape: how much he was part of it, with what keenness he breathed its fragrance, acknowledged its colours, seemed at one with the olive tree over which he ran his hand. It was as if he felt his own body to be part of the body of his country, as if his being flowed out into it and at the same time received it into himself. 'Look,' he said, 'at that light: how it enfolds everything within it, like a womb, or like the sea. You feel that if there were to be a single crack in it anywhere, everything would empty out of it, it would all drain away, and there would be nothing left. And those mountains: do you see how solid they are? Yet they're so fragile you could move them aside with your stick.' And he reached out with his stick as though literally to move them aside, like curtains. 'You see,' he added, 'they're almost human too.' Or again I remember that small enclosed garden at his house high up on the outer slopes of the Stadium in Athens, where he spent the last years of his life. It wasn't larger than the house itself, and he had 'furnished' it much as a shepherd would furnish his hut with familiar objects that seemed to epitomize the Greek land-scape, seemed like emblems of its harsh beauty: stones, pieces of rock, shells, gnarled twists of wood, olive or plane, fragments of marble. It was the Greek world in miniature, an image of a restored paradise; and sitting there with him, especially in the evening, after the cicadas had stopped their chorus and when the air itself had become still, it felt as if those unseen presences that haunt the Greek world had quietly taken up residence in it and were filling it with their benediction. 'My task', Seferis once said, 'is not with abstract ideas but to hear what the things of the world say to me, to discern how they interweave themselves with my soul

97

and with my body, and to express them.' And on another occasion he said: 'I know that all my life I shall never be able to express what I want to express—this union of nature with the simple human body.'

Yet he does express it. Time and again in his poetry this sense of the intimate relationship between man and nature, of the one belonging to the other and even in some way of the one *being* the other—time and again this sense is conveyed in his poetry. It is conveyed, for instance, in the following poem, 'Sleep wrapped you in green leaves', also from his early work *Mythistorima*. Here indeed the sense that nature participates in the movements and perplexities of man's own life is so vivid that nature itself, the physical world, appears like another human being, like a living presence:

Sleep wrapped you in green leaves like a tree
you breathed like a tree in the quiet light
in the limpid spring I watched your face:
eyelids closed, eyelashes brushing the water.
In the soft grass my fingers found your fingers
I held your pulse a moment
and felt your heart's pain in another place.

Under the plane-tree, near the water, among laurel
    sleep moved you and scattered you
around me, near me, without my being able to touch the
    whole of you—
one as you were with your silence;
seeing your shadow grow and diminish,
lose itself in the other shadows, in the other
world that let you go yet held you back.

(37)

I do not want to give the impression that Seferis was simply an elemental person, or a primitive, or a child of nature. He may have been to a certain extent all of these. But he was also and above all a human being. This may sound a rather trite thing to say. We all think of ourselves as human beings. We tend to take it for granted that this is the case. On the other hand we seldom think of what it means to be a

98

human being, or of the obligations and responsibilities which it demands. To begin with, very few of us possess the art of being ourselves. We are usually acting out some part, some image of ourselves, of what we would like to be or, if we occupy a public office, of what we are expected to be or of what others would like us to be. In this way there is usually something artificial and unnatural about us. Instead of being what we are we try to put across this falsified picture of ourselves which we have chosen or which we have accepted. And to the degree to which we are successful in doing this we cease to be human beings. Or at least we cease to be human beings in the way that was true for Seferis.

Seferis was one of those rare people—and they are rare, much rarer than one tends to think—who do not try to be other than they are, or who have the humility to be what they are. I say 'humility', because that is what it is: generally one likes to give an impression of being better than one is. He was one of those rare people who are without affectation, who are entirely natural and capable of being themselves. I think it may have been this quality which made his company so refreshing: because he was himself unaffected, he induced a similar naturalness in other people: they felt that they too did not have to pretend to be other than they were. And he combined with this another great quality: the quality of sympathy, of warm human sympathy, of being open and receptive to other people, of never being patronizing or superior or aloof, of never judging unkindly but of trying always to heal and encourage through understanding and compassion.

Of course these qualities—qualities of simplicity, directness, lack of affectation—do not always come easily to a person. They have to be won, and often behind them lies much pain and suffering. Basically they come from a kind of inner freedom, from what we might call a capacity for spontaneity. Only one must be careful in saying this. We have recently developed the idea that spontaneity is the opposite to discipline—that it is a freedom from restraint, something which someone achieves by merely doing what he or she wants to do. This has had a disastrous effect in most spheres of life, and nowhere more so than in the sphere of art, and particularly perhaps in the sphere of poetry. It has to do with the feeling that you can dispense with a knowledge of your craft and that all you need is to be sincere and true to your emotions, and to express these as violently and vividly and directly as possible, and you will have produced a work of art. And perhaps behind this feeling lies another: that an artist does not really need to know anything, or to study anything, or to be educated in the proper sense of the word; that art can go with an arrogant anti-intellectualism. Somewhere Dostoievsky speaks of the passionate intensity of the young of his generation, of how they are ready to fling themselves into political action and are ready to die for a cause or an ideology; and of how not one of them is ready to make that sacrifice which really counts, that devotion of several years of life to trying to discover, through study of the monuments of art and intellect, what he or she truly is and what is worth doing when once one has penetrated beneath the surface of things. It is still the same for many who call themselves artists in the present generation: they have not been through the labour of learning, the study of their craft, and their work in consequence has the wrong kind of spontaneity and naturalness—not the kind that makes art, whatever else it may make.

I say this because those qualities of which I spoke —qualities of simplicity, directness, lack of affect-ation—typify not only Seferis as a man but also his poetry. Of course, the poetry reflects the man. But what it is important to realize is that these qualities of Seferis' poetry were not just automatic. They were the reward of long years of study and discipline. Seferis' first work—*Strofi*—was published in 1931, when the poet himself was thirty-one. But he had been writing poetry since his early 'teens and by the time he was twenty had recognized that his life's work was to be a poet. And throughout those long years between the ages of eighteen and thirty he gave all his available hours to the study and refinement of his 'poetics', to learning the tools of his craft. It was not an easy task. 'The ghastly situation of the young in Greece who want to write', he notes in his diary written during this period:

There is no one to guide them. There is not even a basic book to teach them the language. The ethical climate is totally negative. There are no elders. They tell you: turn to the Greek earth, to the Greek village, there you will find our true life. Excellent. But in the meantime the young have to live somehow; and I ask myself how, when neither the soil nor the village gives them enough to live on.

And a little later he adds:

I write as one who cuts his veins open. I write in order to postpone a confession. Each piece of writing is for me like the suspension of a punishment . . . If one could only die. I feel myself to be sick. I can't control my heart, or my thought—I can only just control what I write. I don't know how to love any longer, I don't know how to admire anything. I'm a sick creature, total affliction.

He must during this period have written hundreds of poems. But none of them was what he wanted and he rejected them all. I think one of the great lessons that Seferis has to teach is this one of the poet's apprenticeship: his relentless, assiduous, devoted pursuit of his craft. Because it demonstrates that those qualities which typify his poetry as they typify all good art, are the fulfilment of a long discipline, an ascetic discipline as it might be called. There is no royal road to poetry or to any other art.

It is the same where these qualities in a person are concerned: that inner freedom, spontaneity and simplicity which we associate with the most mature kind of person, above all with the saints, are also the fulfilment of a long discipline, a long ascetic discipline. Seferis' life was a long study in learning to be human. As I said, we are often not so aware of the demands and responsibilities of being human as we should be. Seferis was extremely aware of them. They were a continual preoccupation with him, a continual concern. He knew how hard it was to preserve the human measure and he saw all round him those who had failed to keep it: those who tried to be more than human, who set themselves up as supermen, self-appointed saviours or makers of history even, and those who became less than human, who became sub-human. As Seferis saw things, one could sin against the human measure in these two ways. One could try to be more than human, one could try to be a kind of superman: that was one way. Only if one did that, Seferis insisted, one invited one's own destruction. He saw this as an almost natural law, on the model of that law enunciated by Heracleitus: 'The sun must not overstep its measure; if it does, the Furies, ministers of justice, will track it down.' The same fate awaits those, Seferis concluded, who overstep the human measure, or who try to overstep it: the Furies, the ministers of justice, will eventually track them down.

The second way in which one could sin against the human measure was by falling below it, by becoming less than human, by becoming sub-human. This was the fate of those who, in Seferis' words, 'fail to respect the light which God gives each day'. Symbolically he saw this type of person represented in those companions of Odysseus who failed to respect the Sun: those who killed and ate the Sun's cattle and who were punished for their crime by being sent to Hades. He wrote of them, half whimsically, half seriously, in an early poem:

> Since we still had some hardtack
> what stupidity
> to eat while on shore
> the Sun's slow cattle,
>
> for each was a castle
> you'd have to battle
> forty years and become
> a hero and a star.
>
> On earth's back we hungered,
> but when we'd eaten well
> we fell to these lower regions
> mindless and satisfied.

(407)

'Perhaps you will ask me why I write about (this type of) person with sympathy', he once said. And he went on: 'Because the men who belong to this category . . . are the most sympathetic. Even the Homeric Odysseus, when he sees (one of them) . . . among the dead, pities him and sheds tears. I do not say they are lovable or admirable. (They) symbolize those to whom we refer in our daily conversation with the expression: "the poor devil". However,' he concludes, 'let us not forget that these guileless men, precisely because they are "easy", are often the best carriers of evil which has its source elsewhere.' And in another poem he returns to this theme of the bewilderment of a human being when he sees that his 'companions'—whoever they are: fellow-countrymen, friends, or even all mankind—have failed to live up to the measure of man and have somehow ceased to be human:

> . . . I don't understand these faces I don't understand them,
> sometimes they imitate death and then again
> they gleam with the low life of a glow-worm
> with a limited effort, hopeless,
> squeezed between two wrinkles,
> between two stained café tables;
> they kill one another, grow smaller,
> stick like postage stamps to window panes—
> the faces of the other tribe.
>
> We walked together, shared bread and sleep
> tasted the same bitterness of parting
> built our houses with what stones we had
> set out in ships, knew exile, returned
> found our women waiting—
> they scarcely knew us, no one knows us.
> And the companions wore statues, wore the naked
> empty chairs of autumn, and the companions
> destroyed their own faces: I don't understand them.

(169)

But, it may be asked, did he have no ideology, this man, no political creed or religious beliefs? These are difficult questions. As we have seen, he affirmed that his task was not with abstract ideas; and elsewhere he remarked: 'I have no idea about philosophical positions or world views . . . I don't like people who try to express world views in writing poetry.' Yet in practice, of course, it is not so simple: one cannot escape from one's ideas about things, however naive or misguided these may be. But where politics at least are concerned, I do not think I am being unjust to Seferis' memory when I say that he had no political creed and belonged to no particular political party. He himself testifies to this, and to his own attitude. 'I began to sense my isolation from the world of Greek party politics fairly early on—from the end of the 1935 movement', he wrote in 1967.

> I underline the word 'party'. . . . And now, after passing a whole life rocked by military movements, dictatorships, political changes, uprisings, destructions and disappointments—after living through all this, in the flesh, as I might put it, as a civil servant, I find it sad and burdensome to conclude that over all these years we have not made the slightest step forward in these matters. And when a country does not show any change for the better in forty years, this means that it is falling headlong. . . . Speaking as I do speak, I have in mind all the party structures, from the extreme right to the extreme left, however they manifest themselves. I do not blame the institutions and the political systems; I blame the lunacy in us which makes us degrade every institution and every system, and to smother our activities with rhetoric. . . . 'But surely we must give our help?' it will be asked. Of course we must. I'm not in a position to proclaim general canons of behaviour. But personally I believe that one helps better by performing the task that God has given one to perform during our short existence as honourably and as excellently as one can. Not by nourishing the party turmoil.

Seferis' own task was to be an artist. And he once asked himself the question: what should an artist do in the face of the political fanaticisms of our time? Should he give himself to a political cause—by helping, for instance, to combat those political systems to which he feels hostile or by helping to support those of which he approves? Seferis' own answer was that an artist should remain independent of politics—that he should give himself to his art and that this art should be as it were autonomous. This doesn't mean that he felt that the artist should be politically irresponsible. It means that he felt that the artist's duty was to be true to himself: true not just to his superficial self, his private likes and dislikes, but to his most profound self, there at the roots of his being where he is linked by the most sensitive fibres to the world in which he lives, to the most intimate thoughts and feelings of the people among whom he dwells. In expressing his most profound self and in being loyal to that, the artist will therefore at the same time be expressing the aspirations, the anguish, the joy and the humiliations of that part of humanity which encompasses him. 'The great artist', it has been said, 'is not *of* his time. He *is* his time.' But, Seferis went on, the artist cannot carry out this task unless he is left free to carry it out. It is as simple as that: constraint of the artist is constraint of his art. It is therefore inevitable that the artist—the true artist—simply through expressing himself in his art is at the centre of the struggle for human liberty wherever this is threatened or crippled. It cannot be otherwise.

At this point it may be objected that on at least two occasions Seferis appears to have abandoned this principle of political non-commitment and to have put his authority and his poetry at the service of a political cause. In 1955, Seferis published a volume of poems dedicated to 'the people of Cyprus, in memory and love'. It was at the time when much of the Greek-Cypriot population felt that the British were frustrating its legitimate desire to take charge of its own affairs; and Seferis' publication of a volume of poems dedicated to the people of Cyprus just at this time, and containing poems written in Cyprus, was taken by some to signify that Seferis was at last dressing himself in the mantle of a national poet and espousing a national cause; it was taken by others to indicate that he was abandoning his high idea of the poet's function and was beginning to write what was little more than political propaganda in verse form.

I do not think either assumption was correct. Seferis was

105

neither adopting the rôle of a national poet nor writing propaganda. He was in fact continuing to be true to his principles; and when in Cyprus he felt that a foreign power was crippling the self-expression of the Greek-Cypriot people—when in the words of one of his masters, General Makriyannis, he felt that injustice was stifling justice—it was inevitable that this feeling should be reflected in some of the poetry he wrote then. And the situation was still more bitter for him because this same foreign power was that with which he, along with so many of his fellow-countrymen, had co-operated during the long years of a war fought precisely for this right of self-expression; and he was indebted and linked to this power in so many ways, through so many personal friendships. The bitterness of this situation comes through, for instance, in the following poem, one of those in the Cyprus volume, and the one written perhaps with this sense of a betrayal by an ally most in mind. It is almost as if it were addressed to his English friends. He calls it 'Salamis in Cyprus':

Sometimes the midday sun, sometimes handfuls of light rain
and the beach covered with fragments of ancient jars.
The columns insignificant; only the ruined church of
    St Epiphanios

revealing—dark, sunken—the might of the golden Empire.

Young bodies, loved and loving, have passed by here;
throbbing breasts, shells rose-pink, feet
fearlessly skimming the water,
and arms open for the coupling of desire.
The Lord upon many waters,
here upon this crossing.

Then I heard footsteps on the stones.
I didn't see any faces; they'd gone by the time I turned.
But the voice, heavy like the tread of oxen,
remained there in the sky's veins, in the sea's roll
over the pebbles, again and again:

'Earth has no handles
for them to shoulder her and carry her off,
nor can they, however thirsty,

sweeten the sea with half a dram of water.
And those bodies,
formed of a clay they know not,
have souls.
They gather tools to change them;
they won't succeed: they'll only unmake them
if souls can be unmade.
Wheat doesn't take long to ripen,
it doesn't take much time
for the yeast of bitterness to rise,
it doesn't take much time
for evil to raise its head,
and the sick mind emptying
doesn't take much time
to fill with madness:
there is an island . . .'

Friends from the other war,
on this deserted and cloudy beach
I think of you as the day turns—
those who fell fighting and those who fell years
    after the battle,
those who saw dawn through the mist of death
or, in wild solitude beneath the stars,
felt upon them the huge dark eyes
of total disaster;
and those again who prayed
when flaming steel sawed the ships:
'Lord, help us to keep in mind
the causes of this slaughter:
greed, dishonesty, selfishness,
the desiccation of love;
Lord, help us to root these out . . .'

—Now, on this pebbled beach, it's better to forget;
talking doesn't do any good;
who can change the attitude of those with power?
Who can make himself heard?
Each dreams separately without hearing anyone else's
    nightmare.

—True. But the messenger moves swiftly
and however long his journey, he'll bring

to those who tried to shackle the Hellespont
the terrible news from Salamis.

Voice of the Lord upon the waters.
There is an island.

(377)

The second occasion on which it might be said that Seferis
had abandoned his principle of political non-commitment
was in March 1969, when he made his statement about the
military régime in his own country. 'Long ago,' he said, 'I
resolved to remain out of the country's internal
politics. . . . But now for some months I have felt, within
me and around me, that more and more it is becoming
imperative for me to speak out on our present situation . . .'
And he went on again to speak of the shackling of freedom
in Greece, of the denial of basic human liberty—the liberty
to express what is within one, so crucial for an artist above
all—and of the tragedy that 'waits at the end, inescapably,
for dictatorial régimes that seem to have such an easy beginning.' And he concluded: 'I am a man completely without political ties and I speak without fear and without passion.'

Again, in spite of Seferis' avowal that he was a man without political ties, this statement has been taken as an
indication that he had become politically committed. He had
not. But he was humanly committed. He was committed to
this value of the integrity of the human being—to his sense
that this integrity must not be violated, whatever the reason
given or the excuses made, however good or convincing they
may appear. And he was committed to this because unless
the artist is allowed to be true to himself and to express what
is true to himself, he cannot function as an artist. And in
some measure, Seferis would have said, every human being is
an artist. Unless one understands the artist's fundamental
need to be 'true to himself' one cannot understand why his
art must always be an affirmation of human freedom and
why he himself in some way always becomes a symbol of that
freedom. If Seferis' funeral was a national occasion—which
it was—this was precisely because he, a non-political man,

had become a symbol of that personal freedom for which we always long.

What, though, of the other question? Did Seferis hold beliefs that one might call religious? This is perhaps a more difficult question. Of course, Seferis was born into a world in which the great spiritual and liturgical tradition of the Orthodox Church was, so to speak, as much part of the Greek landscape as the mountains or the sea; and his childhood was nourished by the images and symbols of this tradition which animates by its presence every corner of that landscape. Later, these images and symbols from the Christian tradition were to be joined by those of the pre-Christian world, for these too, in another and perhaps more remote, less actual sense, animate every corner of the Greek landscape; and the heroic dignity and heroic suffering of some of the figures of this ancient world—of Odysseus or Oedipus or Socrates—became for Seferis types of the same passion as that lived by the Christian Saviour, especially as this is represented in what Seferis was to call 'the most sublime form of spring I know', the Easter services of the Orthodox Church. So powerful in Greece is this myth of the wounded God who dies and is born again that, as another Greek writer puts it, when you walk in a Greek village at Easter behind the Epitafio, breathing in the air the first scents of spring, you can then sense how close the buried Christ is to the small brother of Persephone. And Seferis himself used to say how difficult it was for him to distinguish whether the figure being buried was that of Christ or Adonis. Born and brought up in the environment of a living and great tradition, Seferis, from instinct and perhaps unconsciously, wove the events of his life and of the life around him together within a framework of a mythical vision so closely that, as in the case of the ancient Greek dramatists, it is difficult to separate the mythical elements in his poetry from the 'plot' itself.

Then, as we have already remarked, Seferis had this very vivid sense of the physical world—an almost primitive sense. He felt very closely related to the living things about him; he

109

had a profound intimacy with them. That wedge which rapid and uncontrolled mechanization inserts between man's soul and his natural environment had not penetrated very deeply into him. Platonic thought has played a greater part in the Greek East than Aristotelian thought, and I think that this is not unconnected with a particular sense of the natural world—a sense which, to use a much abused term, one might call pantheistic. This is a sense that nature—the created world, including man's own physical existence—is rooted in the metaphysical world and as a consequence is capable of sharing in the highest functions of life. It is a sense that man should harmonize himself with the natural world and respect it, rather than set himself apart from it or rather than subject the natural world to some discipline, scientific or economic, which he can only do on condition that he cuts himself off from his natural roots. 'I have a very organic feeling', wrote Seferis, 'that identifies human life with the natural world of Greece.' Seferis, I think, would have reciprocated the advice of the Japanese poet, Bashō: 'Go to the pine if you want to learn about the pine, or to the bamboo if you want to learn about the bamboo. And in doing so, you must leave your subjective preoccupation with yourself. Otherwise you impose yourself on the object and do not learn. Your poetry issues of its own accord when you and the object have become one—when you have plunged deep enough into the object to see something like a hidden glimmering there. However well phrased your poetry may be, if your feeling is not natural—if the object and you are separate—then your poetry is not true poetry but merely your subjective counterfeit.' Within Seferis' poetry is this perception that man, trees, flowers, mountains and rivers have each their own particular consciousness and vitality and that each share in the life of all and are the life of all. Human struggle is continued in the elements of nature, and man draws his own energy from the same sources as those from which every other natural form draws it. Rooting his images always more deeply in life, in the Greek world, Seferis seems to be in continual search of these inner sources of vitality—sources

which everyday preoccupations so easily obscure and over-
lay:

> Bend if you can to the dark sea forgetting
> the flute's sound on naked feet
> that trod your sleep in the other, the sunken life . . .
>
> (63)

he writes in his poem 'Santorini'; and later in the same poem
he adds:

> free yourself from unfaithful time
> and sink . . .
>
> (64)

And these sources Seferis seems to experience as personal
powers, living realities:

> . . . Voices out of the stone out of sleep
> deeper here where the world darkens,
> memory of toil rooted in the rhythm
> beaten upon the earth by feet
> forgotten.
> Bodies sunk into the foundations
> of the other time, naked. Eyes
> fixed, fixed on a point
> that you can't make out, much as you want to:
> the soul
> that struggles to become your own soul.
>
> (69)

Also in the poetry there seems to be a sense of some deep
loss, as if man's life has been torn with violence from its
natural setting whose peace and tenderness haunts him and
fills him with unbearable nostalgia. It is a sense that might be
compared to the experience of an uprooted plant that, still
bleeding at its roots, remembers how it once belonged to the
earth and still mourns for its old garden:

> . . . I'm looking for my old garden;
> the trees come to my waist
> and the hills resemble terraces
> yet as a child

111

I used to play on the grass
under the great shadows
and I would run for hours
breathless over the slopes.

(215)

Of course, it is quite possible to identify this sense of loss
and dispossession with events in Seferis' own life. From
between about the ages of eighteen and twenty-six Seferis
was in Paris, studying. They were very lonely years, and the
loneliness at times almost destroyed him. They were also
years in which he suffered a double ordeal. The first—which
he suffered at a distance, it is true, but no less on that
account—was what has become known as the Asia Minor
disaster: the defeat, in 1922, of the Greek forces in Asia
Minor by the Turks, the burning of Seferis' hometown,
Smyrna ('The Greeks say it was the Turks who burned down
Smyrna,' Seferis was later to write, 'the Turks say it was the
Greeks. Who will discover the truth?' The wrong has been
committed. The important thing is: who will redeem it?'),
and the subsequent exchange of populations which meant the
expulsion of virtually all the Greeks from Anatolia: the up-
rooting, that is to say, of a people from a homeland they and
their ancestors had occupied for three thousand years or
more. How can one measure the impact of such a loss, either
in group terms or in terms of an individual as sensitive and as
conscious of his heritage as the young Seferis—this complete
rupture with the past, with the world of one's childhood, the
total disappearance of so much that one has been identified
with, or has identified oneself with? Then, during the latter
part of this long period and extending forward for several
further years, Seferis lived through a deep but ultimately
ruptured erotic relationship—an experience which is
reflected in his long poem 'Erotikos Logos', that profound
lament for this second loss of what in some way must have
been identified for him with the possibility of personal
happiness, of personal fulfilment.

There is no doubt that this double ordeal and this double
loss cast their influence over the whole of Seferis' life and

poetry. It is as if something seminal and grave had broken in the depths of his being—as indeed it seems to have broken in the heart of the whole epoch, since many of the great poems of the 1920s—Neruda's *Residencia en la tierra*, Alberti's *Sobre los angelos*, Lorca's *Poeta en Neuva York*, Eliot's *The Waste Land*—also speak of this spiritual crisis: this sense of a disintegrating world, a world dissolving under one's gaze into a kind of modern death dance, a world in which matter and mankind seem equally undone: 'Shape without form, shade without colour/Paralysed force, gesture without motion', as Eliot put it. Yet from this crisis in consciousness, or season in hell, Seferis emerged, wounded, full of anguish and nostalgia, but aware as never before of the complex reality compelling both his confrontation and his understanding. It was from this confrontation and understanding that were born all the poems which Seferis wrote during the 1930s, from 'Mythistorima' down to 'The King of Asine'. All convey this sense of ordeal and loss—of a homeland lost, of the loss of that human presence in whom alone life seemed to hold out some prospect of happines and benediction:

> . . . And the poet lingers, looking at the stones, and asks
>   himself
> does there really exist
> among these ruined lines, edges, points, hollows and curves
> does there really exist
> here where one meets the path of rain, wind and ruin
> does there exist the movement of the face, shape of the
>   tenderness
> of those who have shrunk so strangely in our lives,
> those who remained the shadow of waves and thoughts
>   with the sea's boundlessness
> or perhaps no, nothing is left but the weight
> the nostalgia of the weight of a living existence
> there where we now remain unsubstantial, bending
> like the branches of a terrible willow-tree heaped in the
>   permanence of despair. . . .

(261)

Yet this nostalgia, which begins perhaps in some quite

113

personal emotional experience, may end with the meta-physical experience of an Oedipus who, after much suffering, after many blind journeys, descends at last living into the earth 'that receives him mercifully' and returns him to the Great Mother of Rebirth.

For finally what I would say lies at the heart of Seferis' poetry is this sense of a rebirth, of the possibility of everything being renewed, of a resurrection or a transfiguration. It is a continual aspiration, a continual expectation, even in the midst of the torment, the degradation and the suffering which always seem to surround human life: 'And I with only a reed in my hands', he writes in one of his later poems, 'Memory II':

And I with only a reed in my hands.
The night was deserted, the moon waning,
earth smelled of the last rain.
I whispered: memory hurts wherever you touch it,
there's only a little sky, there's no more sea,
what they kill by day they carry away in carts and dump behind
   the ridge.

I was fingering this pipe absent-mindedly;
an old shepherd gave it to me because I said good-evening to
   him.
The others have abolished every kind of greeting:
they wake, shave, and start the day's work of slaughter
as one prunes or operates, methodically and without passion;
sorrow's dead like Patroclus, and no one makes a mistake.

I thought of playing a tune and then I felt ashamed in front of
   the other world
the one that watches me from beyond the night from within
   my light
woven of living bodies, naked hearts
and love that belongs to the Furies
as it belongs to man and to stone and to water and to grass
and to the animal that looks straight into the eye of its
   approaching death.

So I continued along the dark path
and turned into my garden and dug and buried the reed

114

and again I whispered: some morning the resurrection will
    come,
dawn's light will blossom red as trees glow in spring,
the sea will be born again, and the wave will again fling forth
    Aphrodite.
We are the seed that dies. And I entered my empty house.

(357)

Sometimes, too, this sense of a resurrection is so strong and
actual that it happens before the poet's eyes. For a moment
the normal processes and activities of the world come to a
halt, everything is suspended—as it was at the birth of
Christ—and the miracle occurs: this miracle in which human
life is caught up into some other, more rich and radiant life.
He writes of this sudden vision of a transfiguration in
another fairly late poem, 'Engomi':

Broad the plain and level; from a distance you could see
arms circling as they dug.
In the sky, the clouds all curves, here and there
a trumpet golden and rose: the sunset.
In the meagre grass and the thorns
stirred light after-shower air: it had rained
there on the peaks of the mountains that now took on
    colour.

And I moved on towards those at work,
women and men digging with picks in trenches.
It was an ancient city; walls, streets, and houses
stood out like the petrified muscles of cyclopes,
the anatomy of spent strength under the eye
of the archaeologist, anaesthetist, or surgeon.
Phantoms and fabrics, luxury and lips, buried
and the curtains of pain spread wide open
to reveal, naked and indifferent, the tomb.

And I looked up towards those at work,
the stretched shoulders and the arms that struck
this dead silence with a rhythm heavy and swift
as though the wheel of fate were passing through the ruins.

115

Suddenly I was walking and did not walk
I looked at the flying birds, and they had stopped stone dead
I looked at the sky's air, and it was full of wonder
I looked at the bodies labouring, and they were still
and among them the light bringing forth a face.
The black hair spilled over the collar, the eyebrows
had the motion of a swallow's wings, the nostrils
arched above the lips, and the body
emerged from the struggling arms stripped
with the unripe breasts of the Virgin,
a motionless dance.

And I lowered my eyes to look all around:
girls kneaded, but they didn't touch the dough
women spun, but the spindles didn't turn
lambs were being watered, but their tongues hung still
above green waters that seemed asleep
and the ploughman stood fixed with his staff poised.
And I looked again at that body ascending;
people had gathered like ants,
and they struck her with lances but didn't wound her.
Her belly now shone like the moon
and I thought the sky was the womb
that bore her and now took her back, mother and child:
Her feet stayed marble still
and vanished: an Assumption. . . .

(385)

On other occasions, this longing for resurrection was so
strong that it pierced through even the curtain of physical
death itself—pierced through and saw life in death. Some
years before his death, at the funeral of a friend in Athens, as
the coffin was being lowered into the grave, the lid slipped
and exposed the dead man lying there; and Seferis suddenly
gripped the arm of the person he was with and pointed in
excitement to the dead man in the grave: 'There,' he said,
'there is the resurrection.' And a few days before his own
death, as he was lying in the ward in the hospital, a young
girl was wheeled into the ward and placed beside him, she
also close to her death; and the poet, who for days had been
motionless, as though in a coma, suddenly now turned his

head and gazed at her with wide unmoving eyes. Perhaps through her dying form he was even in his own death seeing the lineaments of her transfigured form, reborn in the light, as he had seen that of Antigone in the final lines of his long poem, 'Thrush':

Light, angelic and black,
laughter of waves on the sea's highways,
tear-stained laughter,
the old suppliant looks at you
as he's about to cross the invisible fields—
light mirrored in his blood . . .
Sing little Antigone, sing, O sing . . .
I'm not speaking to you about things past, I'm speaking about
    love;
decorate your hair with the sun's thorn,
dark girl;
the heart of the Scorpion has set,
the tyrant within man has gone,
and all the daughters of the sea, Nereids, Graeae,
hurry to the radiance of the rising goddess:
whoever has never loved will love,
in the light.

(331)

The Figure of Aretousa

(from the seventeenth-century Cretan epic *Erotokritos*)

Now it is over. The courtiers have made their last bows, the trumpets have stopped sounding and the lances have been put to rest against the wall. The nurse goes back to her knitting, the birds to their trees, the mountains to their stations by the sea. King and queen retire into dignified old age, and the lovers whose passion we have witnessed vanish from our sight. All these characters, their masks of anonymity lowered, have moved for a time before our eyes, vivid *dramatis personae* of a mediaeval pageant. Now they have disappeared to take up their ordinary rôles once more, to continue somewhere behind the scenes the business of living. And what remains? What image has joined itself to our life?

Gradually, when the book is closed, the epic loses its dramatic quality, its quality of action. The dialogue becomes a monologue, the monologue itself condenses into something much finer, something more pure and uncontaminated: condenses into the portrait of a person free from the accident of time and place. The honest, brave Erotokritos; the king in his wrath; the weeping, faithful nurse Frosyni; Polidoros, the councillor, and his wife in their senility and loneliness—these are contributory figures, leading up to the main figure. They act as mirrors, they suffer. But their suffering, real as it is, personal as it is, does not end in themselves. They are true beings, but at the same time they are parts of a larger, more significant being. They are borne along in the flow of the verse, they rise from it, they sink back into it; and they surrender at last, as the poem itself surrenders at last, to a single image, to an image in which they, and the poem with

118

them, not only achieve themselves, not only realize their destinies, but are also, in the very act of fulfilling themselves, at the same time transcended.

In the end, from the strong current of the verse that turns the dialogue by which the poem is broken into a monologue, into a continuous lyric utterance; from the flowing in and the flowing out of the tide which at every turn throws up a new event, another person, only to suck all events, all persons, back into the depths; in the end, from the up and down of the waves, from the final surge of the waters, rises the figure of Aretousa: the transfiguration of a personal drama, an image of the human soul.

It is difficult to think of another figure in literature with whom one might compare Aretousa. There are of course other figures who share with her certain individual characteristics. There is Antigone, for instance. Antigone possesses the same devotion, the same innocence; but her love is the love of a sister, although of a sister for whom all men of the world are brothers. Or there is Juliet. Yet, in spite of its beauty and intensity, Juliet's love still has about it the sense of something held in glass, as if what Juliet loved was an image of herself or a reflection in a mirror. Even Dante's Beatrice, translated by death in childhood, seems more the idealized object of an unconsummated passion than a living, breathing woman.

It is not simply that in Aretousa we watch the planting and growth of the delicate seed of love, the overflowing into the human soul of a diffuse power which seizes with irresistible gentleness all the forces of mind and body when they abandon themselves to it. That, no doubt, is part of the story. But if it were all, then we should have not *Erotokritos* but a pastoral idyll like that other Cretan work, the *Voskopoula*, sophisticated and touching perhaps, but altogether lacking the dynamic strength of the poem of Kornaros. No, what is surprising, and what distinguishes *Erotokritos* from other works whose plot it may resemble, is the quality of Aretousa's love. There is absolutely nothing disembodied about it. It is rooted at the centre of her being.

In spite of her youth, her love is adult, not adolescent. Also it is uncompromising, it takes account of nothing but itself. Even if only because it was a literary convention, yet it is fitting that Kornaros gave his poem a pre-Christian setting, for its tone is more archaic than Christian. There was in the love of that age something direct, something instinctive whose force seems later to have been tamed. It is as if this love was still a power of nature and nothing more. It is as if it was neither good nor bad, but was simply a blind force working irresistibly to achieve its object.

It is something of this quality that the love of Aretousa possesses. Although *Erotokritos* is in the tradition of the songs of courtly love written by the Provençal lyrist-lovers, it belongs to a different world. The refinements of the courtly lover, his truth, his courtesy, his loyalty, are certainly present in *Erotokritos*. But they are subordinate. Set beside the naked force of the love which gives the poem its great impetus, they hardly count; they vanish far into the background. Aretousa aspires with her whole being to union with the beloved, and between her and this union no obstacle is to stand, whatever its nature, not even the obstacle of death. For even if death should come between her and her lover, then:

> What our bodies have not done, our souls shall do in Hades.
>
> (V.1048)

Aretousa's love is an erotic love in the true sense of the word. It is a love which has its object both in the visible and in the invisible world and which, focused on a human person, is yet able to break through the limits of the purely mortal to affirm itself on the other side of death.

If Erotokritos is the lover, Eros is the *daimon* of Aretousa. But this Eros is not the meek boy, the plaything of Venus: this is not the Eros of *Erotokritos*. The Eros of *Erotokritos* is rather the fierce Serpent, armed with fire and arrows, of

Apuleius: a power that flies by night, fastens onto the soul of man and grips it like a vampire. Eros is an ancient terror, an avenger, one of the dark gods. Woe to her whom he chooses as a victim! For then she is no longer herself, she no longer controls her own actions, she is the instrument of a god, she is possessed. And possession of this kind has in it a madness, a disequilibrium of mind and body that devastates all logic and against which law, custom, morality, the will of the father, the will of the mother, the welfare of the state are as nothing.

The progress of Eros in the human soul may culminate in ecstasy, but the way of Eros is the way of destruction. He is a fiery power, remorseless, daimonic:

> O Rose, thou art sick:
> The invisible worm
> That flies in the night,
> In the howling storm,
> Has found out thy bed
> Of crimson joy:
> And his dark, secret love
> Does thy life destroy.
>
> (Blake, 'The Sick Rose')

Eros: the 'invisible worm', the destroyer of life. But Eros is also the bringer of life. Eros works through sacrifice, but it is the sacrifice which leads to the resurrection.

The sacred fire burns in Aretousa. It burns and consumes her. She is no longer Aretousa, the daughter of a king, obedient to the conventions and ceremonies of palace life. She is the instrument in the power of something stronger than herself. Like Phèdre she might cry out:

> Ce n'est plus une ardeur dans mes veines cachée:
> C'est Venus toute entière à sa proie attachée.

For it is possession by some similar power that Aretousa knows:

> Eros frenzies me, how can I forsake him.
>
> (I.1662)

121

Or later:

> Honour, paternal fear, bind me and restrain me.
> And on the other side Eros has so wounded me,
> That I do not know who will be the victor.
>
> (III.216-8)

Or again:

> You understand how Eros shoots into the heart,
> Becomes its lord and master, seeks its inner bed,
> And no one can resist him, no one can escape.
>
> (III.249-51)

This power which seizes Aretousa robs her of her ordinary self; but at the same time it enables her to become more herself, more Aretousa, more the royal daughter, more a woman. Eros, this pure desire, is an energy between the divine and mortal worlds. He mingles with the human, subjugates it, ennobles it, compels it towards actions which in the common light of day would paralyse it with fear and terror.

Once Eros has been received, the more he is denied, the more he exerts himself; and the more he exerts himself, the further he drives his human victim towards the extremes of existence, towards that inner transformation without which human destiny cannot be fulfilled.

When the Lord spoke to Abraham 'Get thee out of thy country, and from thy kindred, and from thy father's house, unto a land that I will show thee', Abraham did not ask where that land was, or why he must go, or how he was to get there, or what was to be the purpose of the journey. He simply 'departed, as the Lord had spoken unto him', trusting that his journey would end in the Promised Land.

So it is with Aretousa. When Eros has spoken to her, she does not ask whether what Eros has commanded is right or wrong, or where it will lead her, or if it is worthwhile. She obeys. But her obedience is not the obedience of a slave to his master; it is not obedience to some external impersonal

122

power. What she obeys is the voice that speaks at the heart of her own being. Her actions spring from a depth in the human psyche where the distinction between what commands and what obeys is obliterated. In fulfilling what she is commanded, Aretousa fulfils herself; and it is she who commands. 'I am Heathcliff', says Catherine in *Wuthering Heights*. So might Aretousa say: 'I am Erotokritos'; for, as she does say: 'Erotokritos is Eros' (III.253). There is, in love of this kind, no distinction between the love itself, the person who loves and the person who is loved. Yet, although the three are one, the one does not obliterate the separate identities of the three.

Lastly, what a large part darkness and night play in this drama! It is in the night that Aretousa first hears the songs of her unknown lover. It is in the night that she first speaks to Erotokritos, through the grille of a cellar window. It is in the night of the prison that she waits for five years for Erotokritos to come back.

The night of the prison: Danaë in her tower, Eurydice in Hades, Mary Magdalene at the mouth of the sepulchre, Juliet in her tomb, Aretousa in the night of the prison: women who wait, wait for deliverance: images of the human soul's longing for release.

Perhaps after all the theme of *Erotokritos* is freedom, the struggle for freedom. Love and freedom: are they not interconnected? The songs which Aretousa hears plant within her the seed of love. But, we are told, if the seed is to flourish, it has first to die. There must be the tearing apart, the sundering, the crucifixion. Erotokritos must be exiled, must wander in a far country; Aretousa must be held in prison, ignorant whether her lover is dead or alive, but no more able to renounce her love than she is able to renounce herself. For a time the anger of the king must triumph, there must be the bitter period of desolation and bondage. The return of Erotokritos is the return of love. It is also the return of freedom. The country is saved, the wrath is brought to an end, there is the great promise of reconciliation. And if when Erotokritos does come back, disguised, his first message to Aretousa, who has waited five years in prison for him, is to tell her that he is dead and that she will never see him again, this is not merely because he has a sadist's desire to test whether she is 'faithful unto death'. It is because a love of this kind, if it is to perfect itself, must pass through a moment of final despair, of furthest separation, of complete abandonment: for it is this death which precedes the deliverance, it is this that makes possible the beginning of the new life.

References

INTRODUCTION

1. Robert Byron, *The Byzantine Achievement* (London, 1929), p.7.
2. Lord Byron, *Childe Harold's Pilgrimage,* Canto 11, LXXXVIII.
3. H. W. Nevinson, 'Beyond the Law' in *Visions and Memories* (London, 1945), p.5.
4. Virginia Woolf, 'On Not Knowing Greek', *The Common Reader* (London, 1925), pp.39, 54–5.
5. Robert Byron, *op. cit.* p.17.
6. For a full account of this development, see R. R. Bolgar, *The Classical Heritage* (Cambridge, 1933).
7. George Finlay, *A History of Greece* (Oxford, 1877), vol. VI, p.28.
8. George Finlay, *op. cit.* p.40.
9. Robert Byron, *op. cit.* p.9.
10. W. R. Lethaby and H. Swainson, *The Church of Sancta Sophia* (London, 1894).
11. O. M. Dalton, *Byzantine Art and Archaeology* (Oxford, 1911).
12. D. H. Lawrence, 'The Greeks are Coming' in *The Complete Poems of D. H. Lawrence* (London, 1964), vol. 2, p.687.
13. Lawrence Durrell, *Reflections on a Marine Venus* (London, 1960), p.183.

ANDREAS KALVOS AND THE EIGHTEENTH-CENTURY ETHOS

1. For details of Kalvos' life see R. Gartagani, *Andreas Kalvos Apanta* (Athens, 1960). The original Greek texts of Kalvos' poems on which my translations given here are based are also to be found in this book.
2. See Edward John Trelawny, *Records of Shelley, Byron and the Author* (Penguin Books, 1973), pp.125–6.
3. Thomas Gray, 'Ode on the Death of a Favourite Cat'.
4. Thomas Gray, 'Ode on a Distant Prospect of Eton College'.

125

5. Cited in R. Gartagani, *op. cit.* p.65.
6. Henry Holland, *Travels in the Ionian Islands, Albania, Thessaly, Macedonia etc.* (London, 1815), pp.12-25.
7. Thomas Traherne, *The Centuries*, III, 3.
8. George Seferis, 'Prologos yia mia ekdosi ton "Odon" ', *Dokimes* (Athens, 1962), pp. 160-1.

GENERAL MAKRIYANNIS: THE PORTRAIT OF A GREEK

1. See Strategou Makriyanni, *Apomnimonevmata*, second edition (Athens, 1947). An English translation of part of this work has been made by H. Lidderdale: see *Makriyanni* (London, 1966). The translations quoted here are my own.
2.

ANGHELOS SIKELIANOS AND HIS VISION OF GREECE

1. Anghelos Sikelianos, 'I Elevsineia Diathiki', *Nea Grammata 2* (Athens, 1936), p.52. All translations, except as noted, are my own.
2. See T. Dimopoulos, *O 'Dithyramvos tou Rodou' tou Sikelianou* (Athens, 1934), p.118.
3. Anghelos Sikelianos, *Anoikto Ypomnima sti Megaleiotita Tou* (Athens, 1922), *passim*.
4. Anghelos Sikelianos, 'I Elevsineia Diathiki', *op. cit.* pp.59-60.
5. Anghelos Sikelianos, *Anoikto Ypomnima sti Megaleiotita Tou*, p.3.
6. *Ibid.*
7. Anghelos Sikelianos, 'I Elevsineia Diathiki', *op. cit.* p.47.
8. Anghelos Sikelianos, *Kostis Palamas* (Athens, 1943), p.41.
9. Anghelos Sikelianos, 'I Elevsineia Diathiki', *op. cit.* p.51.
10. Anghelos Sikelianos, *I Delfiki Enosi* (Athens, 1932), p.12.
11. Anghelos Sikelianos, 'Ellinikes Pnevmatikes Axies', *Nea Estia* vol. 29 (Athens, 1941), p.10.
12. Anghelos Sikelianos, 'Eisagogi sto kallitekniko ergo tou Conrad Westpfahl kai to poiitiko tis Kas Westpfahl', *O Kyklos*, Year 4 no. 5 (Athens, 1937), pp.141-2.
13. Anghelos Sikelianos, 'John Keats', *Anglo-Greek Review* vol. 2 no. 11 (Athens, 1947), p.349.
14. Anghelos Sikelianos, 'Eisagogi sto kallitekniko ergo tou Conrad Westpfahl', *op. cit.* p.139.
15. Anghelos Sikelianos, *I Delfiki Enosi*, pp.10-17.
16. Anghelos Sikelianos, 'I Elevsineia Diathiki', *op. cit.* p.140.

17. Cited by T. Dimopoulos, *op. cit.* p.112.
18. E. R. Dodds, *Humanism and Technique in Greek Studies* (Oxford, 1936), p.11.
19. See W. K. C. Guthrie, *Orpheus and Greek Religion* (London, 1935), *passim*; Plato, *Phaedo*, 69c etc.
20. Herodotus IV, 95.
21. N. K. Chadwick, *Poetry and Prophecy* (Cambridge, 1942), p.102.
22. *Ibid.*
23. Aurobindo Ghosh, cited in S. Radhakrishnan, *Indian Philosophy*, vol. I (Oxford, 1927), pp.69–70.
24. Aristoxenos, cited in F. M. Cornford, 'Mysticism and Science in Pythagorean Tradition', *The Classical Quarterly* XVI, 3–4 (London, 1922), p.142.
25. T. Gomperz, *Greek Thinkers*, trans. L. Magnus (London, 1901), vol. I, p.127.
26. H. G. Rawlinson, *The Legacy of India* (Oxford, 1937), p.5.
27. S. Radhakrishnan, *Eastern Religions and Western Thought* (Oxford, 1939), p.143.
28. Anghelos Sikelianos, 'John Keats', *op. cit.* p.347.
29. *Ibid.*, p.347.
30. Anghelos Sikelianos, 'I Zoi kai to Ergo tou Pindarou', *Anglo-Greek Review*, vol. 3 no. 7 (Athens, 1947), p.196.
31. N. K. Chadwick, *Poetry and Prophecy*, p.14.
32. Anghelos Sikelianos, 'I Zoi kai to Ergo tou Pindarou', *op. cit.* p.194.
33. *Ibid.*, p.195.
34. Anghelos Sikelianos, 'I Elevsineia Diathiki', *op. cit.* p.52.
35. Anghelos Sikelianos, 'Aeschylus', *Anglo-Greek Review*, vol. 5 no. 7 (Athens, 1951), p.258.
36. See Anghelos Sikelianos, 'Eisagogi sto kallitekniko ergo tou Conrad Westpfahl', *op. cit.* p.141.
37. Anghelos Sikelianos, 'I Zoi kai to Ergo tou Pindarou', *op. cit.* p.194.
38. Anghelos Sikelianos, 'Aeschylus', *ibid.*
39. Anghelos Sikelianos, 'I Zoi kai to Ergo tou Pindarou', *op. cit.* p.196.
40. Anghelos Sikelianos, 'Prologos tou "Lyrikou Viou" ', *Nea Estia* no. 336 (Athens, 1942), p.842.
41. Anghelos Sikelianos, cited in T. Dimopoulos, *op. cit.* p.116.
42. Anghelos Sikelianos, *I Delfiki Enosi*, p.9.
43. See Philip Sherrard, 'Anghelos Sikelianos' in *The Marble Threshing Floor* (London, 1956), pp.125–83.
44. Friedrich Hölderlin, *Hyperion*, trans. William R. Trask (New York and Toronto, 1965), p.32.

1. All quotations from Seferis' poetry are from his *Collected Poems 1924-1955*, translated, edited and introduced by Edmund Keeley and Philip Sherrard (London, 1969). The number in brackets after each quotation refers to the page in that work on which the quotation is to be found.